Right Here, Right Now

Carey Scott

Right Here, Right Now

Devotions for Women

180 READINGS FOR BUSY DAYS

ISBN 979-8-89151-154-5

Cover design by Greg Jackson, Thinkpen Design

Published by Barbour Publishing, Inc., 1810 Barbour Drive, Uhrichsville, Ohio 44683, www.barbourbooks.com

Our mission is to inspire the world with the life-changing message of the Bible.

Printed in China.

Yes, life is busy—but that should be no barrier to time spent with God.

These devotions are perfect for women on the go, offering brief, thought-provoking entries that can be read

- on an airplane
- in a restaurant
- hiking the trail
- between classes
- lying in bed
- awaiting an appointment. . .
- right here, right now!

In 180 entries written by and for women, *Right Here, Right Now Devotions for Women* will inspire you to keep God in your thoughts amid the activity and stress of daily life.

Featuring scriptures from the fresh-yet-familiar Barbour Simplified KJV Bible, these devotions will challenge you to a greater knowledge of God—and commitment to Him.

Created for Community

And let us consider one another to provoke to love and to good works, not giving up the assembling of ourselves together, as is the manner of some, but exhorting one another, and so much the more as you see the Day approaching.

HEBREWS 10:24–25

Life's busy, often making it super challenging to fit church into the mix. With work and school commitments, responsibilities to family and friends, and the need to care for your own physical and mental well-being, consistency at church can easily fall down the priority list. But this isn't God's desire.

Scripture tells us not to forsake getting together because community is important. God created you to thrive in Christian community, because it's how you offer and receive encouragement. It helps to strengthen the resolve to be faithful. And it helps us—together—keep our eyes on Him through every season. While the trend may be slacking off to gain "me time," why not buck the trend and make church a commitment no matter what?

What can I do, right here, right now, to deepen my commitment to church?

He Held Nothing Back

"For God so loved the world that He gave His only begotten Son, that whoever believes in Him should not perish but have everlasting life."

JOHN 3:16

Imagine someone you don't yet know, loving you so perfectly they'd willingly sacrifice their son to save you from the eternal consequences of your sins. It seems unimaginable, but that's exactly what God did for you.

You may deeply love your friends and family, but never enough to offer up your child as payment for their wrongdoing. You may go to the mat for them when facing hardship, but always with limits. You may be their ride-or-die, but there's a line you just wouldn't cross.

God, through His Son Jesus, held nothing back. He exceeded every limit and crossed every line. Through Christ's death on the cross, He gave it all for you. He made a way to save you from yourself and find forgiveness and redemption for eternity.

What can I do, right here, right now, to recognize how deeply God loves me?

Gut Punches

My brothers, count it all joy when you fall into various temptations, knowing this, that the testing of your faith works patience.

James 1:2–3

Is James saying you should be happy when life punches you in the gut? No, friend, he is not. Instead, he's asking you to shift your perspective from the earthly to the eternal. He's challenging you to consider every hardship from God's perspective, remembering His steadfast love. And James wants you to fully trust that the Lord only allows these gut punches if they're for your ultimate good.

You can trust God only has your best in mind as He grows your faith through messy moments and draining difficulties. A hardship doesn't mean God is mad at you. He isn't looking for ways to trip you up. The truth is that He knows the end game. He allows discomfort and discouragement now because it will produce goodness and grit later. And that is why you can count each gut punch as joy.

What can I do, right here, right now, to shift perspective on my struggles?

Peace Through Prayer

Be anxious for nothing, but in everything, by prayer and supplication with thanksgiving, let your requests be made known to God. And the peace of God, which passes all understanding, shall guard your hearts and minds through Christ Jesus.

PHILIPPIANS 4:6–7

You cannot always fix your problems. Even if you're highly educated, terribly clever, or full of life experiences, you're still limited by your human condition. But God is not. In His sovereignty, He understands every detail of your circumstances. He gets why you're discouraged and why the situation feels overwhelming. He knows all the unknowns that keep you tangled up. So, trying to tackle worry and fear in your own strength only sets you up for more of the same.

God's desire is for your anxious heart to find peace—the kind the world simply cannot offer or grasp. In prayer, unpack every stress, every time it stirs you up. Ask for His help. And find lasting rest from those anxious thoughts.

What can I do, right here, right now, to pursue a peaceful heart?

God's Consistency

"Heaven and earth shall pass away,
but My words shall not pass away."
MATTHEW 24:35

Everything in this world, both the good and the bad, is temporary. Be it that killer new job, a group of good and godly friends, an exciting travel schedule, or a calendar packed with family fun, the reality is that these won't last forever. Fortunately, the stress from relationships, the grief from loss, or the heartache from unmet expectations won't either.

For a believer, these are all momentary experiences because this isn't her final home. Scripture clearly says everything here is fleeting. It will pass away. But God's words will not.

That means you can cling to Jesus and trust He's eternal. His promises are unwavering. His love is unrelenting. His wisdom is unchanging. His goodness is unsurpassed. And as you keep your eyes trained on Him, you will find stability. Let scripture be the firm foundation that provides much-needed consistency in a world that's always changing.

What can I do, right here, right now,
to let God's words steady my heart?

It's Faith Alone

For by grace you are saved through faith,
and that not of yourselves; it is the gift of God,
not of works, lest any man should boast.
EPHESIANS 2:8–9

Paul is setting the record straight, so we don't adopt wrong thinking. Some people believe it's good intentions that secure a place in heaven. They assume thoughtful actions and kind words toward others earn an eternal home with God. And while we may live in a world that drives us to work harder and smarter to get ahead, the truth is that's not how God's economy operates.

It is faith in Jesus that saves. There's nothing you can personally do to ensure a heavenly home except trust in Him alone. God sent Jesus here to restore the relationship that sin broke, and it was the only thing that could accomplish the task. It's the gift that keeps giving, forever.

What can I do, right here,
right now, to understand eternity
can't be secured by my actions?

The Discipline to Grow

And every man who strives for victory has self-control in all things. Now those do it to obtain a corruptible crown, but we, an incorruptible crown. So I run, therefore, not with uncertainty. So I fight, not as one who beats the air, but I discipline my body and bring it into subjection, lest that by any means, when I have preached to others, I myself should be disqualified.

1 Corinthians 9:25–27

Think of the self-discipline a professional athlete must have to be a true competitor in their sport. They spend crazy amounts of time focused on building strength and stamina so they can bring their best to every competition. It's required if they're going to succeed.

As believers, Paul is suggesting we need to have the same mindset and regimen. We need to train in ways that grow us spiritually so we can weather any storm that comes our way. Be intentional to let your faith be active every day.

What can I do, right here, right now, to strengthen my faith?

You're No Accident

"For I know the thoughts that I think toward you," says the Lord, *"thoughts of peace and not of evil, to give you an expected end. Then you shall call on Me and you shall go and pray to Me, and I will listen to you. And you shall seek Me and find Me, when you shall search for Me with all your heart."*

Jeremiah 29:11–13

God created you on purpose and for a purpose. He took time to plan and intentionally made you just as you are. He baked in the skills and talents needed for your calling, and even determined when on the kingdom calendar you'd come into the world. You're no accident.

As you grow in faith and discover God's plan, He'll meet with you as you pray for guidance. When you seek Him in the Word, you'll find Him. Life may be busy with everything on your plate, but don't miss the real reason God has you here, now.

What can I do, right here, right now, to understand my purpose?

Biblical Joy and Peace

Now may the God of hope fill you with all joy and peace in believing, that you may abound in hope through the power of the Holy Spirit.

ROMANS 15:13

It's important to remember that God is the source of hope. Your busy day may be overwhelming and unpredictable with career, family, and friends, but He will steady your anxious heart and keep you anticipating His goodness. Even more, the Lord will supernaturally fill you with His joy and peace in the midst of it. Sound impossible?

Let's remember that biblical joy isn't the same as worldly happiness, because it's not dependent on our circumstances. It's dependent on knowing God. And experiencing biblical peace isn't dependent on an absence of conflict. Instead, peace comes from having a robust relationship with the Lord.

Hope, joy, and peace work together divinely in the heart of believers. They produce a confidence that God loves you and will meet you in the messiness in meaningful ways.

What can I do, right here, right now, to embrace biblical joy over worldly happiness?

God's Abundance

Have you not known? Have you not heard that the everlasting God, the Lord, *the Creator of the ends of the earth, does not faint, nor is weary? There is no searching of His understanding. He gives power to the faint, and He increases the strength of those who have no might.*

Isaiah 40:28–29

There are days that just plain exhaust us from sunup to sundown. There are relationships that make us weary and hopeless that things will ever improve. Our careers demand our best, even when our best is deeply lacking that week. But our loving and generous God will give us what we need in every challenging moment.

What do you need today? Energy to finish the project? Patience to deal with difficult people? Strength for a hard conversation? Insight for better understanding? Let it comfort your heart that God never grows weary and cannot lose strength. And when you ask Him for help, He will give generously.

What can I do, right here, right now, to let God recharge me?

The Goodness of God's Word

All scripture is given by inspiration of God and is profitable for doctrine, for reproof, for correction, for instruction in righteousness, that the man of God may be perfect, thoroughly furnished for all good works.

2 Timothy 3:16–17

The Bible is good for believers. It's useful and essential. And as we navigate a life of faith in the Lord, it serves a divine purpose. It teaches, rebukes, corrects, and shows us how to live in a right relationship with God. It teaches us how to better manage our time and finances. It helps us with relationships and parenting. It highlights what needs to change in our life and encourages us to ask God for help.

Your life may be full, but choose to set aside time and dig into scripture daily. Every time you do, God will meet you in its pages in meaningful ways. Your spirit will be refreshed, and the roots of your faith will deepen.

What can I do, right here, right now, to prioritize reading my Bible?

Your Faith Pleases God

But without faith it is impossible to please Him, for he who comes to God must believe that He is, and that He is a rewarder of those who diligently seek Him.

HEBREWS 11:6

Why is it impossible to please God without faith? Because faith is how you anchor your trust in His promises. It's how you secure your eternity in heaven. It's what enables you to have confidence in who He is, knowing He'll act on your behalf. It's how you go from head knowledge of God to heart knowledge. Faith is how you connect with the Lord and seek His wisdom and guidance.

Your faith pleases God, because through it, you're empowered to live for Him and embrace the calling placed on your life. Faith secures your identity as a child of God. And as you lean on God throughout your packed day, He delights to give you what is needed to conquer it.

What can I do, right here, right now, to live out my faith?

Asking in Prayer

"Therefore I say to you, whatever things you desire when you pray, believe that you receive them, and you shall have them."

Mark 11:24

God is not a genie, and He never promises that whatever we want will be ours. Because of His love, the Lord won't give you something that is short-sighted, hurtful, or inappropriate. He won't go against His character to grant your request just to make you happy.

You may want your boss to take a hike or your bank account to magically fill up or a relationship that isn't good for you to flourish. And while you are always welcome to ask God for your heart's desire, you can trust He'll only answer in ways that are good for you.

Why not ask Him to make you love what He loves? Then, as your heart aligns with His, your prayers and petitions will naturally follow.

What can I do, right here, right now, to pray with a pure heart?

Keeping Anger in Check

He who has no rule over his own spirit is like a city that is broken down and without walls.

PROVERBS 25:28

While God created us to have a range of emotions, we're to control them with His help rather than allowing them to control us. Anger is one emotion that often takes over at a moment's notice. The flight was late, and we missed an important event. Someone was unkind to our child. We weren't selected for the program or project. Someone deeply offended us. And within a moment, our temper flares.

The truth is there's good anger—righteous anger—that's appropriately directed toward sin. But too often, the anger we experience is rooted in selfishness, and others pay for it. When that emotion begins to rise in you, pray. Ask God to give peace and perspective. And let Him show you the next right step so you can keep your anger in check.

What can I do, right here, right now, to appropriately manage my temper?

Working It All Together

And we know that all things work together for good to those who love God, to those who are the called according to His purpose.

Romans 8:28

As a believer, you can trust with confidence that regardless of what you're facing today, God is working. He's not only making sure everything comes together for your good, but He's also working it together for His glory.

That means you can know the Lord is with you in the mess. You can exhale with certainty because He's involved in the details of your circumstances. Let today's verse bring steadfast assurance that He is at work, even if you can't see it quite yet. It may not end in the ways you think are best, but God will work things together according to His will and timing, which always bring blessings to those who love Him. Friend, nothing can stop God's plans for you.

What can I do, right here, right now, to trust that the Lord is always at work in my life?

Making Church a Priority

Let the word of Christ dwell in you richly in all wisdom, teaching and admonishing one another in psalms and hymns and spiritual songs, singing with grace in your hearts to the Lord.

Colossians 3:16

Your faith is not meant to be expressed privately—at least not exclusively. There may be moments where you hide away with God in prayer to seek His comfort and peace. You may have times of personal praise and worship on your lunch break or in your car. Or your time alone in the Word may be a daily discipline. But being together with other believers in a church setting has great value.

Make corporate teaching and worship a priority. Your work week may have been long, your daily schedule grueling, your family responsibilities challenging, and your personal tasks tiring. . .but something supernatural happens when believers meet together.

What can I do, right here, right now, to make church a non-negotiable?

Recall and Rejoice

Rejoice in the Lord always, and again I say, rejoice.
PHILIPPIANS 4:4

Sometimes joy feels like something you deeply long for but just can't seem to grasp. There are often too many earthly struggles that keep you from fully or completely experiencing it. And while your faith in God may be solid, navigating each day with joy just isn't something you're able to do.

Why not shift your eyes from your struggles to your Savior? It's easy to focus on an overwhelming to-do list and forget God's goodness. When dealing with a challenging career or a cranky child or a grueling travel schedule, remembering His perfect provision can be tough. Life has a way of robbing our contentment. But scripture says to *always* rejoice in God because there's *always* something worth praising Him for!

Think back to those times where He's blessed you. When feeling down, recall and rejoice.

What can I do, right here, right now, to remember God's goodness when I'm stretched thin?

The Divine Purpose

And not only so, but we also glory in tribulations,
knowing that tribulation works patience,
and patience experience, and experience hope.
ROMANS 5:3–4

Becoming a believer in Jesus doesn't make you immune to life's trials and tribulations. Have you ever wondered why not? Why wouldn't God promise His followers an existence that was easy and free from heartache?

The truth is that every challenge we face has a divine purpose, even the one you're walking through right now. We only grow through adversity. And you can trust that He only allows these difficulties if they'll eventually be for your good and His glory. You see, God plays the long game. He's more interested in growing your faith than ensuring your comfort. And the Lord will use every opportunity to deepen your roots in Him as He prepares and equips you to live out the calling on your life each day.

What can I do, right here, right now, to trust God's purpose in my tribulations?

The Trinity

"I am Alpha and Omega, the beginning and the ending," says the Lord, "who is, and who was, and who is to come, the Almighty."

Revelation 1:8

This profound statement by Jesus speaks volumes about how the Trinity works. By saying He's the Alpha and Omega, it means He was there in the beginning as Creator and will also be there at the end as Conqueror. This is a reference to Him being God, as the second member of the Trinity.

Hebrews 12:2 tells us Christ is the author and finisher of our faith. And several places in the book of Isaiah reference Him as the first and the last, clearly recognizing the eternal nature of the Godhead. When Jesus said He is the Alpha and Omega, it revealed He's the God of both the Old and New Testaments. While it may be confusing at times, we can trust that the Trinity is three in one, and above all else earthly or heavenly.

What can I do, right here, right now, to better understand and appreciate the Trinity?

Hope Comes from Scripture

For whatever things were written formerly were written for our learning, that through patience and comfort from the scriptures we might have hope.

Romans 15:4

In this world, we all need hope. You may need it right now more than ever. Your job may feel unstable. There may be a health issue that makes you nervous. Finances might be a huge stressor. A key relationship may seem shaky, at best. And we're all facing a future of unknowns. Hope for a good outcome is what keeps us going day after day.

The problem is that too often, we look to the wrong things for security. We place our faith in worldly options that promise to deliver, but only offer temporary or shallow hope. But God knows your needs, friend. And scripture is how He speaks. When you choose to dig into the Bible seeking the hope it guarantees, your heart will be comforted and encouraged with confident expectation.

What can I do, right here, right now, to find hope that settles my anxious heart?

Faith Comes by Hearing

*But they have not all obeyed the gospel.
For Isaiah says, "Lord, who has believed
our report?" So then faith comes by hearing,
and hearing by the word of God.*

ROMANS 10:16–17

The gospel message is what saves. And for that to happen, it must be received to be believed. Not everyone who hears the gospel, however, will ultimately become a believer. We all have free will to accept or reject Jesus as Savior. But unless there's an opportunity, salvation most certainly won't happen. So we know hearing—be it through listening to or reading the gospel message—precedes saving faith.

What is the gospel message? That Jesus came into the world to be the payment for our sins. He paid our debt in full through His death on the cross. He was buried and rose on the third day. When we believe this message, our faith leads to eternal salvation.

What can I do, right here, right now, to ensure my salvation in heaven?

The Spirit Intercedes

Likewise the Spirit also helps our infirmities. For we do not know what we should pray for as we ought, but the Spirit Himself makes intercession for us with groanings that cannot be uttered. And He who searches the hearts knows what the mind of the Spirit is, because He makes intercession for the saints according to the will of God.

Romans 8:26–27

What a relief to know that the Holy Spirit has complete knowledge of every detail of your circumstances. When you can't find the words to pray or have no idea what to ask for, He intercedes on your behalf because He fully understands. In your career or personal life, you may feel pressure to always have the right words at the right moment, but when you pray to God, that pressure should fade—you don't need to speak perfectly.

There's enough stress in life between work and home. Don't avoid praying simply because you don't know what to say. The Holy Spirit wants to intercede on your behalf.

What can I do, right here, right now, to pray with confidence?

Your God-Given Ability

For God has given us a spirit not of fear but of power and of love and of a sound mind.
2 Timothy 1:7

Did you know that Paul wrote this letter from jail, awaiting execution? Even in his last days, he was thinking about encouraging Timothy, knowing the task of leading Jesus' church in sharing the gospel would soon be on his shoulders. Timothy, a young man, needed a reminder to be strong, to not give in to the tendency to be timid. He needed self-discipline, which is careful and sensible thinking to move forward.

But Paul's encouragement is for you too. You're also called to leadership in your own life. And God has given you the ability to have discernment so you can make the right choices. You can decide to implement well-disciplined habits in your day and stick to them. You can lead with purpose and passion. With God's help, you can stand strong and choose well.

What can I do, right here, right now, to be led by self-discipline?

Sharing the Gospel

And Jesus came and spoke to them, saying, "All power has been given to Me in heaven and on earth. Therefore go and teach all nations, baptizing them in the name of the Father and of the Son and of the Holy Spirit, teaching them to observe all the things that I have commanded you."

MATTHEW 28:18–20

Jesus commanded His disciples to spread the good news, teaching them how to live in right relationship with God. It was a powerful call to continue carrying forward all they had been taught. And they weren't alone! They'd be empowered and equipped to do the work set before them.

You may feel scared to share the gospel with others. You might feel like there's just no time to have gospel conversations or answer endless questions. You may not want to risk offending people in your life. But as believers, we're called to spread the gospel when God opens the door. Ask for eyes to see opportunities and courage to speak up.

What can I do, right here, right now, to prepare my heart to share the gospel?

The Right Church

I was glad when they said to me,
"Let us go into the house of the Lord."
Psalm 122:1

At the end of a long week and in preparation for another tough one, sometimes it's hard to get excited about church. Maybe it's your only chance to sleep in or it's a day to catch up on what you couldn't get done earlier. And rather than looking forward to corporate worship and a powerful message, church feels like just another thing on your to-do list.

But when you're at the right church, it can be a place of restoration to the weary soul. It can become the most cherished time of the week, knowing the time with God's people will provide good support and much-needed encouragement to manage whatever's coming. And the time with believers will allow you to serve and be served, letting your heart be filled in meaningful ways.

Be committed to finding a church that preaches the full counsel of God, and then joyfully invest in it weekly.

What can I do, right here, right now, to find—or support—the right church?

Fullness of Joy

You will show me the path of life.
In Your presence is fullness of joy; at Your right hand there are pleasures forevermore.
PSALM 16:11

Where do you look for joy? Is it in earning a solid performance review and a raise? In finally finishing a tough project or task? Does your joy come from frequent travel for vacation or a full social schedule with your friends? Maybe it's from buying something you've always wanted or hitting a milestone in your workout plan? While there's nothing wrong with any of these, let's remember that worldly joy is fleeting. It's here one day and gone the next.

Scripture says we can only find the fullness of joy—the kind that is true and lasting—by spending time in God's presence. It's realizing we're loved no matter what. It's knowing our eternity is secure with Him. It's experiencing His goodness every day. And that kind of joy is constant and unaffected by life's ups and downs.

What can I do, right here, right now, to find lasting joy in God?

Endurance for the Hard Seasons

Blessed is the man who endures temptation, for when he is tested, he shall receive the crown of life that the Lord has promised to those who love Him.

James 1:12

When faced with struggles and challenges, how do you respond? Do you ignore them, hoping they'll just go away? Do they knock you to your knees, making it hard to find your footing again? Maybe you hide away and binge-watch TV or pour yourself into work so as not to deal with your feelings. Or maybe you become obsessed with fixing everything yourself.

God wants you to stand strong in faith and persevere through those times. This is when you dig into scripture for encouragement. It's when you connect with godly friends who can support your journey. These are the times you pray continually for strength and wisdom. And when you do, there's a beautiful blessing from God on the other side.

What can I do, right here, right now, to strengthen my faith to endure hard seasons?

Your Unchanging God

"For I am the Lord*; I do not change.*
Therefore you sons of Jacob are not consumed."
Malachi 3:6

In a world that changes all the time, what a blessing to know that God never changes. He is right now who He has always been, and He will remain the same forever. God cannot be changed. Nothing can sway His goodness and compassion. His promises will not falter. His love is steadfast and dependable. And the commands in the Bible are still designed to bless and guide your walk of faith. Let this give you stability and peace.

Your heavenly Father is dependable in every way, so lean on Him when you need a firm foundation. Dig into His Word when you need direction that is both timely and relevant. And pray when you're desperate for steadiness to settle your anxious heart. God will not change, and that is a true gift for every believer.

What can I do, right here, right now,
to find peace and rest in God's stability?

God's Word Has Purpose

"For as the rain and the snow come down from heaven and do not return there but water the earth and make it bring forth and bud, that it may give seed to the sower and bread to the eater, so shall My word be that goes out of My mouth. It shall not return to Me void, but it shall accomplish what I please and it shall prosper in the thing for which I sent it."

ISAIAH 55:10–11

God's Word has a purpose. There's reason for every verse in the Bible. And while written by men, the entire library of scripture—Genesis to Revelation—is God-breathed and divinely inspired. Knowing His Word will not return void encourages us to be in it regularly because of its power to transform the human heart.

We can trust the Word to do exactly what God wants it to accomplish. It may be unpredictable for us, but the Lord's will always comes to pass.

What can I do, right here, right now, to believe in the power of God's Word?

Faith That Moves

And answering, Jesus said to them, "Have faith in God. For truly I say to you that whoever shall say to this mountain, 'Be removed and be cast into the sea,' and shall not doubt in his heart but shall believe that those things that he says shall come to pass, he shall have whatever he says."

MARK 11:22–23

Most likely, Jesus wasn't saying that words spoken in faith can literally move mountains. Nor is He saying that if we have enough faith, everything we want will be ours. Instead, Jesus is alluding to the big obstacles and overwhelming situations we all face. It's our faith in God that empowers us to stand with boldness, relying on His strength and wisdom to clear those obstacles from our path.

There's no guarantee that the illness will heal, the relationship will be restored, the workload will decrease, or the busyness of life will end. But if our prayers for movement are in God's will, they will move.

What can I do, right here, right now, to trust God's plans?

Checking Motives

"But you, when you pray, enter into your closet, and when you have shut your door, pray to your Father who is in secret. And your Father who sees in secret shall reward you openly."

MATTHEW 6:6

As believers, we should resist any and every urge to express our faith in order to make ourselves look more holy. We shouldn't attempt to show off, so others think we're super-Christians. How we walk out our faith doesn't require the approval or affirmation of anyone except God. Our focus should be to glorify Him, not to promote self.

Of course, we should pray openly at restaurants before meals. And we can and should pray out loud with a friend or coworker who's struggling. We should serve and give as we feel led. But we should always make certain our motives are pure and true—letting these be genuine responses to God's goodness and kindness in our lives.

What can I do, right here, right now, to check the motives driving my expressions of faith?

Making the Right Choices

For the grace of God that brings salvation has appeared to all men, teaching us that, denying ungodliness and worldly lusts, we should live soberly, righteously, and godly in this present world.

Titus 2:11–12

It should be the desire of your heart to live in ways that please God. From the words you speak to the way you act to what you consume through media, let faith be the filter you use to make the right decisions. And while worldly temptations may catch your eye and tug at your heart at times, the pursuit of righteous living should always come out on top.

Where do you need to make better choices? Where have you been pursuing worldly ways that contradict God's best for you? How have you compromised what's right for what's wrong? Now is the perfect time to rededicate your life to righteous and godly living. His heart and His plans for you are always good.

What can I do, right here, right now, to be more intentional in my choices?

Created for Good Works

For we are His workmanship, created in Christ Jesus for good works, which God has before ordained that we should walk in them.

EPHESIANS 2:10

You were created for a purpose. When God designed you, He also planned the good works you would accomplish. You were created to do great things that ultimately point others to the Father in heaven. Don't ever doubt that you matter deeply. Your presence on God's map, on His kingdom calendar—here and now—is important. And there is something unique to you that God has planned, even if you're still trying to figure out what it is.

Throughout your day, as you navigate work and home life, ask the Lord to reveal the good works designed especially for you. Look and listen for His direction. Be sensitive to the Holy Spirit's leading. And then walk in these ways with courage and confidence.

What can I do, right here, right now, to understand the good works God's planned for me?

Gifts to Serve

As every man has received the gift, even so minister the same to one another, as good stewards of the manifold grace of God. If any man speaks, let him speak as though speaking the words of God; if any man ministers, let him do it as with the ability that God gives, that God in all things may be glorified through Jesus Christ, to whom be praise and dominion forever and ever. Amen.

1 Peter 4:10–11

There are countless reasons to be part of a godly community. Scripture says we've been given at least one gift to use in service to other believers. Together, we can minister and encourage one another, and God will be glorified. This is why serving in the church is important.

You don't have to know what your spiritual gifts are before you step out in service. Often, these gifts become clear as you engage with others. Go ahead and get involved and watch how God brings them into focus.

What can I do, right here, right now, to take a faithful step toward service?

The Fruit of Joy

But the fruit of the Spirit is love, joy, peace,
long-suffering, gentleness, goodness, faith, meekness,
self-control. Against such there is no law.

GALATIANS 5:22–23

When you accept Jesus as your Savior, the Holy Spirit dwells within you, working to shape your character. He nurtures the fruit of the Spirit, helping each quality grow and mature in your heart. Joy is one of those qualities.

This joy can manifest in ways that aren't based on circumstances. It's deeper and longer lasting than what this life can offer. It may be joy for the gift of salvation or deliverance from worldly struggles. Or it may be the joy you experience as you spend time in God's presence and recount His goodness. But joy is ultimately a choice. As you choose to embrace the Spirit's work in your life, joy will freely flow regardless of the ups and downs of daily life.

What can I do, right here, right now, to choose joy?

No More Pity Parties

Beloved, do not think it strange concerning the fiery trial that is to test you as though some strange thing happened to you. But rejoice because you are partakers of Christ's sufferings, that when His glory shall be revealed you may be glad also with exceeding joy.

1 PETER 4:12–13

Trials and suffering are part of the human experience; there's no way to avoid them. Even as believers, we know from the Bible that we should expect them. God's Word shows us how to develop a strong and flexible faith muscle, one with the endurance and perseverance to get us through the valleys.

But Peter goes a step further in today's verse by challenging us to shift our perspective. He suggests that instead of having a pity party when the storms come, we should choose to see every hardship as an opportunity to stand in solidarity with Christ. Trials make us participants in His suffering and are powerful opportunities for spiritual growth.

What can I do, right here, right now, to stop feeling sorry for myself?

God Is Perfect

The LORD *is righteous in all His ways*
and holy in all His works.
PSALM 145:17

God is perfect. His ways are always right as He works all things together for the good of those who love Him. It may sometimes feel like the Lord has forgotten you. It might initially seem like He messed up or dropped the ball. You may even decide you know the best way to navigate your future in light of whatever hardship you're experiencing. And while you may be smart, God is infinitely smarter because He knows the ins and outs of every situation. No detail escapes Him. He has full understanding and complete knowledge. He'll never make a mistake. His ways and works are perfect.

So press into God when you're at a crossroads. Ask for divine wisdom and discernment to know the next right step. Trust His guidance, even if it seems counterintuitive. And be quick to thank Him for His goodness when you see it.

What can I do, right here, right now,
to trust God's ways over my own?

God's Word Is Alive

For the word of God is living and powerful and sharper than any two-edged sword, piercing even to the dividing of soul and spirit, and of the joints and marrow, and is a discerner of the thoughts and intentions of the heart.

HEBREWS 4:12

The Bible is not merely a historical book. The writer of Hebrews tells us God's Word is alive and at work in the lives of those who dig into its pages. It's powerful in so many ways, not only offering guidance and wisdom, but also highlighting where we may be falling short. It challenges us to live differently and it unpacks God's commands for righteous living. It brings encouragement by showing how others overcame obstacles and experienced God's goodness. It deepens our faith by revealing the work of the Father, Son, and Holy Spirit.

Even on your busiest day, commit to time in the Word. Pay close attention to every passage. Let the Bible be your handbook for living rightly.

What can I do, right here, right now, to commit to daily Bible reading?

Walking by Faith

Therefore, we are always confident, knowing that while we are at home in the body we are absent from the Lord, for we walk by faith, not by sight.

2 CORINTHIANS 5:6–7

How do you walk by faith and not by sight? Simply stated, it's choosing to navigate life with an eternal focus rather than an earthly one.

It's obeying God's commands when giving in to your own fleshly desires would be easier. It's wanting to please the Lord more than your boss, even when your job is on the line. It's following God's leading, even if your family thinks you're crazy. It's trusting God's commands over your best friend's advice. And it's knowing that by doing these things, your obedience will be rewarded, according to scripture.

Where do you need to refocus and walk by faith today? In the office, at church, or at home? In relationships? In finances? With a scary medical diagnosis? Trust God more than you trust anything or anyone else.

What can I do, right here, right now, to focus on trusting God more?

Praying with Passion

Confess your faults to one another and pray for one another, that you may be healed. The effective fervent prayer of a righteous man avails much.

James 5:16

Prayer is an important part of a believer's walk of faith. And we know through countless scripture references that God hears and answers prayers. So let it be a priority and something you do throughout every day.

You should talk to the Lord when struggling at work, when frustrated in traffic, when roommates or family members are thoughtless, or when feeling stretched by life's responsibilities. You should be quick to pray for those around you who are facing tough times too. And after a hard conversation with someone you love, you should end in a prayer of reconciliation because it brings healing.

Lastly, pray wholeheartedly rather than half-heartedly. Confess sins as you pray with focus and passion. Give God all your attention, and He will answer you.

What can I do, right here, right now, to take prayer more seriously?

Saying No

And those who are Christ's have crucified the flesh with the affections and lusts.

GALATIANS 5:24

Self-control is the ability to say *no* to ourselves. It's choosing God's way over ours. It's showing moderation and restraint when we'd rather do the opposite. It's being balanced and reasonable in our interactions with others.

You can feel the Holy Spirit at work as you're able to control yourself in ways you previously could not.

This is an important part of a believer's life because it helps with the pursuit of righteous living. It empowers you to turn from sin when tempted. It removes the crushing weight of guilt and shame because you're equipped to make godly choices. And it replaces foolishness with faithfulness.

What can I do, right here, right now, to say no to my fleshly desires?

In the Same Measure

"Therefore be merciful, as your Father also is merciful. Do not judge, and you shall not be judged. Do not condemn, and you shall not be condemned. Forgive, and you shall be forgiven. Give, and it shall be given to you."

LUKE 6:36–38

Today's scripture offers a blueprint for the way every believer should live. And at the end of verse 38, Jesus says that with the same measure we do these things, we will receive them back. Yikes! In other words, what we reap we will sow, and in equal measure. So, as we judge our coworkers and condemn family and friends through harsh criticism, we too will be judged. And when we show mercy, forgiveness, and generosity in abundance, we'll experience the same in return.

This is why we need the Lord's strength every day. Overriding our sinful nature isn't always easy. But when asked, He'll give us the ability to heap blessings on others. In return, they'll be heaped on us.

What can I do, right here,
right now, to love others well?

Church Discipline

"For where two or three are gathered together in My name, there I am in the midst of them."
MATTHEW 18:20

At first glance, Matthew 18:20 may seem to be suggesting we need at least two people at a prayer meeting for God's presence to be with us. But what would that mean for believers when praying alone? Is the Lord there too?

This verse is actually about church discipline. It comes right on the heels of instructing believers to confront someone living in blatant sin—with two or three witnesses if necessary. This practice is endorsed by God, but often unpopular in churches because it's hard to do. But when done correctly, God promises to be with us.

Always approach confrontation with a spirit of humility and a desire for reconciliation. Pray and act together. And know that His presence surrounds you.

What can I do, right here, right now, to follow the Word even when it's hard?

The God of Truth

The LORD is near to all those who call on Him, to all who call on Him in truth.

PSALM 145:18

God delights in the truth and expects it from His followers. Isaiah 65:16 says He is the "God of truth." Psalm 119:160 says the entirety of the Bible is truth. And according to Titus 1:2, God never lies. Even the first piece of heavenly armor He provides for believers, helping them to stand against the enemy, is the belt of truth (Ephesians 6:14). Honesty carries weight and matters greatly to God.

So when you're struggling in relationships, are exhausted from a crazy work schedule, or are worried about the future, go right to God with authenticity. Share everything, even the details you'd rather keep hidden. Be sincere about what worries you or creates fear. Just lay it all out there, in truth. . .because He will draw near.

What can I do, right here, right now, to be more honest with God?

Lean on God Instead

Trust in the Lord *with all your heart and do not lean on your own understanding. In all your ways acknowledge Him, and He shall direct your paths. Do not be wise in your own eyes; fear the* Lord *and depart from evil.*

Proverbs 3:5–7

It's hard to *not* lean on your own understanding, especially when you've had some meaningful life experiences to draw from. You've seen your friends and family push through messy moments and come out strong on the other side. Maybe you've gone through therapy, learning to implement healthy boundaries when needed. You may have great ideas and tons of perseverance. But still, God says to trust in Him and not yourself. The truth is that we need our Father's guidance as we navigate the crooked paths of this life.

Be quick to pray when bad news comes. Seek His wisdom when you're confused. Ask for direction. Acknowledge God and He'll direct your next steps.

What can I do, right here, right now, to trust God over my own understanding?

From the Inside Out

A merry heart does good like a medicine,
but a broken spirit dries the bones.
PROVERBS 17:22

Being joyful is key to a happy life and fulfilling relationships. It can even make a challenging job satisfying because you're choosing your attitude, rather than allowing those frustrating circumstances to overwhelm and discourage. A positive outlook is not only good for you but also blesses those around you. Nobody really wants to spend time with Debbie Downer. Amen? And just like medicine, joy can affect every aspect of your well-being and promote healing, from the inside out.

So how can you maintain a merry heart? Find time each day to be in God's Word. Jeremiah 15:16 says, "Your words were found, and I ate them, and Your word was to me the joy and rejoicing of my heart." God will meet you where you are and minister to your weary heart. He will bring encouragement and offer perspective. And He will remind you of His unending love.

What can I do, right here, right now, to choose joy—God's joy?

Trials Are Temporary

But may the God of all grace, who has called us to His eternal glory through Christ Jesus, after you have suffered a while, make you perfect and establish, strengthen, and settle you.

1 PETER 5:10

Peter confirms that, as believers, we will suffer trials and tribulations. It's not an *if*, but a *when*. From receiving insults to experiencing disappointment to facing persecution, we are not exempt from a hard life. We will lose people we love. We will fail at important goals. And we'll face circumstances that result in deep discouragement and pain. While people may argue that a life of faith should be free from difficulties, those are empty words and bad theology.

But there's hope. We can't let ourselves fall into the pit of despair, because no matter what we're experiencing, we know it will be short-lived. This life is temporary, and God is with us as we suffer. He provides strength and guidance along the way, and ultimately much-needed restoration.

What can I do, right here, right now, to persevere with a positive and hopeful attitude?

Nothing Compares

There is no one holy like the Lord, for there is no one besides You, nor is there any rock like our God.

1 Samuel 2:2

Nothing in the world or in the heavens can compare to God. There's no one who can match His goodness or graciousness. He has no counterpart who can compete with His wisdom or strength. There's no rival to His holiness. No one can measure up to His capacity for love. God is first and foremost in every way, all the time, and there's no power or force that can change that powerful truth.

So when you lean into Him as you struggle to meet crucial deadlines, navigate challenging relationships, or work through your endless to-do list, you're putting your faith in the right place. There's no one like God, and He will be your rock in the hard moments. Ask for His help and be confident He will provide it.

What can I do, right here, right now, to put my faith in God above all else?

Meditating on It

"This Book of the Law shall not depart out of your mouth, but you shall meditate on it day and night, that you may observe to do according to all that is written in it, for then you shall make your way prosperous, and then you shall have good success."

Joshua 1:8

If your desire is to live a good life that's righteous and influential in all the right ways, spend time in God's Word every day. The more you read, the more you'll grow in your understanding of who God is and what He promises to do for those who love Him. The truth is you need that knowledge to steady your heart in an exhausting world. As you dig into scripture, you'll be encouraged, and you'll find the strength to keep moving forward.

Meditate on the Word throughout your day. Revisit what you've read and ask God to give peace and revelation.

What can I do, right here, right now, to let God's Word penetrate my heart?

A Better Yes

"For with God nothing shall be impossible."
Luke 1:37

Don't be misled. This verse isn't a sure-fire guarantee that God will always make the impossible happen in your life. Sometimes what you want isn't what He knows is right for you. It may not be the right timing. Or in His sovereignty, the Lord may have a different plan—a better plan—altogether.

So if you're asking for more hours in the day to finish a project, for the man of your dreams to suddenly appear, or for your illness to miraculously vanish, events might not unfold the way you desire. Your prayers may not be answered in the ways you desperately hope. Though the Lord certainly has the ability, He isn't obligated to meet your immediate desire. Believe that He must have a better *yes* down the road. God knows your heart and the desires it holds, and you can trust that He will always do what is best for you. He loves you deeply, you know.

**What can I do, right here, right now,
to trust God's plan more than my own?**

It's a Personal Relationship

"But when you pray, do not use vain repetitions as the heathen do. For they think that they shall be heard for their many words."
MATTHEW 6:7

Let this verse bring freedom to your prayer life. It's an important reminder that there's no formula to follow in your conversations with God. There are no right or wrong ways to share what's on your heart with the Father. Instead, you're invited to speak with authenticity. You can be honest about what's tangling you up emotionally. You can be free to talk about how a key relationship is dragging you down. You can unpack what scares you or stresses you out.

Don't skimp in your prayers, just going through the motions. Don't become repetitious or thoughtless with your requests. Make your personal relationship with God *personal*. He already knows the burdens you carry, but spend time connecting with Him in a meaningful and honest way.

What can I do, right here, right now, to be more real with God in prayer?

Corporate Praise

Praise the Lord. Praise God in His sanctuary; praise Him in the firmament of His power. Praise Him for His mighty acts; praise Him according to His excellent greatness. Praise Him with the sound of the trumpet; praise Him with the lyre and harp. Praise Him with the tambourine and dance; praise Him with stringed instruments and organs.

Psalm 150:1–4

While you can (and should) thank God every day for His goodness, there is something powerful about corporate praise. It is good to be together with other believers, celebrating the Lord as one. Hearing waves of voices raised in worship brings comfort. Hearing testimonies of His help and healing gives strength to the weary. Corporate worship reminds us of our need for God's intervention. It creates space to pray for one another, offering the encouragement that God is still working miracles today.

Yes, life is busy and you're tired. And things may not slow down anytime soon. But make church a priority because your heart needs that togetherness.

What can I do, right here, right now, to look forward to church?

Recipe for Disciplined Living

[A bishop must be] a lover of hospitality, a lover of good men, sober, just, holy, self-controlled, holding fast the faithful word as he has been taught, that he may be able, by sound doctrine, both to exhort and to convince those who contradict.

TITUS 1:8–9

Titus 1:8–9 may be talking about the divine order of the church and those who serve in it, but this recipe for disciplined living is for all of us. As a believer, your choices matter to God. How you walk out faith in your personal life and at work or school is important to Him. And because the goal of life here on earth is to bring God glory through our words and actions, living with intentionality pleases the Lord.

Which description from Titus 1:8–9 is most challenging? Where do you need to refocus? What is the Holy Spirit speaking to you right now? How should you respond? As you go about your day, reconnect with God and recommit yourself to disciplined living.

What can I do, right here, right now, to live with righteous intentions?

Keeping God's Commands

By this we know that we love the children of God: when we love God and keep His commandments. For this is the love of God, that we keep His commandments. And His commandments are not grievous.

1 John 5:2–3

Do you know what God commands of believers? Do you know what His expectations are for those who love Him? If you're not in the Word regularly, there's a good chance you don't know. The Bible is not a book of rules and regulations to enslave, but rather a roadmap to freedom. Keeping His commands sets you up for blessings to flow into your life unhindered and in abundance.

Download an app to your phone or carry a pocket-sized Bible in your backpack, then find moments throughout your day to read God's Word. Take notes on the ways God asks you to obey. And understand there's great purpose in following His will, since it opens doors and unlocks opportunities you may have never imagined.

What can I do, right here, right now, to better know and obey God's commands?

Obedience Unlocks Joy

"If you keep My commandments, you shall abide in My love, even as I have kept My Father's commandments and abide in His love. These things I have spoken to you, that My joy might remain in you, and that your joy might be full."

John 15:10–11

There's an unmistakable connection between obedience and joy. They work together in beautiful ways for the believer. While some people may assume otherwise, following God's will and ways isn't a downer. It's not a weight to bear. And it's not a monotonous or tedious practice. Instead, obeying His commands unlocks your joy.

When you extend grace rather than holding onto an offense, God is pleased. When you are available for Him regardless of a busy day, it delights His heart. As you pursue righteousness in your relationships, the Lord looks on and smiles. Your decision to surrender your will to His every day opens the floodgates of blessing, allowing God's joy to fill your heart to full.

What can I do, right here, right now, to unlock abundant joy?

Conquered Through Him

No temptation has taken you but such as is common to man. But God is faithful, who will not allow you to be tempted above what you are able, but with the temptation will also make a way of escape, that you may be able to bear it.

1 CORINTHIANS 10:13

Being tempted by what the world has to offer is a common thread that knits us together as humans. We are all born with a sinful nature, into a sinful world. Your struggles aren't unique to just you. The truth is that others have battled in the same way. And even in our best efforts, we just can't avoid this struggle with sin. But God uses those desires and cravings to sanctify believers.

Some say the Lord won't give you more than you can handle. That's incorrect. He will never give you more than you can conquer *through His strength*. God will meet you in the temptation and provide a way out.

What can I do, right here, right now, to endure temptations and stand strong in faith?

Nothing Is Too Hard

"Ah, Lord GOD! Behold, You have made the heavens and the earth by Your great power and outstretched arm, and there is nothing too hard for You."

JEREMIAH 32:17

You may not be able to repair a broken relationship, but God can. You may be out of creative ideas for ways to work hard and provide for your family, but He isn't. Maybe you don't have the finances for your start-up, but the Lord has endless resources at His disposal. And while you can't predict the outcome of all your hard work, God knows your next right step. Why? Because there is nothing too hard for Him.

Where are you struggling today? Take heart, friend! You have a heavenly Father who is completely capable in every way. He is fully equipped at all times. And when you lean into Him for help and hope, your faith will result in blessing. Where you can't, God can. Even more, He will.

**What can I do, right here,
right now, to trust God's ability?**

Handle with Care

For I testify to every man who hears the words of the prophecy of this book: If any man adds to these things, God shall add to him the plagues that are written in this book. And if any man takes away from the words of the book of this prophecy, God shall take away his part out of the book of life, and out of the holy city, and from the things that are written in this book.

Revelation 22:18–19

The type of warning included in Revelation 22:18–19 is also mentioned in Deuteronomy 4:1–2 and Proverbs 30:5–6. The takeaway is that no one should tamper with the Word in any way.

Be careful who you listen to. Be mindful of what books you read, if the author has a loose interpretation of scripture. God's Word should never be tweaked to be more palatable or to fit some culturally acceptable narrative. Instead, handle God's Word with awe and admiration. Always seek theologically sound teaching.

What can I do, right here, right now, to protect myself from wrong teaching?

In Him Alone

And my speech and my preaching were not with enticing words of man's wisdom but in demonstration of the Spirit and of power, that your faith should stand not in the wisdom of men but in the power of God.

1 Corinthians 2:4–5

Let's be honest. Too often, we sink our faith into what man can offer. We trust in the promises of our politicians or in the policies of the company we work for. We believe in the words of our favorite professor, assuming every one of them is accurate. We give power to celebrities, being swayed by their opinions and ideas. Or we buy into the narrative from trendy influencers in our area of interest.

The apostle Paul says to put your faith only in God—in His wisdom and power. Our hope should always be only in the Lord. Any person or worldly way of thinking is limited and tainted. But God's way is flawless. Trust in Him alone.

What can I do, right here, right now, to stand in the power of God and not man?

Be an Overcomer

"I have spoken these things to you, that in Me you might have peace. In the world you shall have tribulation, but be of good cheer: I have overcome the world."

John 16:33

The only true and lasting inner peace you can experience is through a robust relationship with Jesus Christ. Rather than depending on ourselves or anyone else to get us through the hard times, it's important we lean on the Lord. He has overcome the things that trip us up in the world.

Jesus gives peace and provision over persecution and problems. He offers success over sin, and a win over worry. Through Him, you can experience triumph over temptation and defeat over discouragement. Be it a hard season at work, challenges at school, struggles in relationships, or some other personal battle, nothing is stronger than Jesus. You may go through difficult times but not without hope. With Christ, you will overcome, because He overcame!

What can I do, right here, right now, to have an eternal perspective on earthly battles?

Don't Give Up

Continue in prayer, and watch in the same with thanksgiving.
COLOSSIANS 4:2

Do you ever feel like giving up when it comes to praying? Maybe it seems like your prayers hit the ceiling and bounce back down. Maybe you feel silly continuing to ask for the same thing over and over again. Or maybe you've grown tired of waiting for an answer. Being persistent in prayer takes steadfast faith and a firm belief that God will answer you.

Friend, don't give up. Continue praying with humility and thanksgiving. Remind the Lord of His promises in the Bible. Remind Him how He's answered in the past—whether in your life or the life of someone you know—and ask Him to do it again. Thank Him for already being at work in your life, even if you can't see it yet. Thank God for being loving and compassionate. And don't grow weary of asking. He cares about what's on your heart.

What can I do, right here, right now, to remain persistent in prayer?

Adding Self-Control

And besides this, giving all diligence, add to your faith, virtue; and to virtue, knowledge; and to knowledge, self-control; and to self-control, patience; and to patience, godliness; and to godliness, brotherly kindness; and to brotherly kindness, love.

2 Peter 1:5–7

As a believer, you have everything you need to live and love well, given by God Himself. You can stand firm in your faith, rejecting the world's ways and walking in righteousness. But don't stop there, friend. Recognize that you're called to *add* godly attributes to your faith, including self-control.

It's important to let the Holy Spirit grow self-control in you. Then you can demonstrate restraint in your work and at home. There may be things you'd like to say that aren't productive. You may want to live without rules. Or you may be quick to respond when you should have taken time to cool down. Ask God to help you master self-control, because it's essential to making life better.

What can I do, right here, right now, to add self-control to my faith?

Hold On to Freedom

Stand fast, therefore, in the liberty by which Christ has made us free, and do not be entangled again with the yoke of bondage.
GALATIANS 5:1

Jesus Christ came to give you freedom from the law. So, as a believer, part of your purpose is to stay free, making sure you don't fall back into old habits and hangups that have entangled you in the past. You get to follow Jesus because you love Him, not because you're required to obey joy-draining rules created and enforced by men. That only brings loads of guilt for making mistakes.

Embrace the freedom you have in Jesus, knowing that your obedience to His will and ways isn't burdensome. It may be challenging to follow at times, but it's ultimately liberating. And there's no condemnation in Christ when you mess up. Remember, your sins have already been forgiven. So, hold on to your freedom by spending time in the Word and in prayer. Connecting with the Lord is key.

What can I do, right here, right now, to hold on to freedom?

The Spirit of Unity

Now may the God of patience and consolation grant you to be like-minded toward one another, according to Christ Jesus, that with one mind and one mouth you may glorify God, even the Father of our Lord Jesus Christ.

Romans 15:5–6

God desires a spirit of unity in the church, and that demands a great deal of patience. It's choosing to love others, even when that's challenging. It's thinking the best of those around you while exercising godly discernment. It means you are humble, understanding the need to be open to other ideas and opinions. It also means that you speak up when you feel led. And honestly, it takes persistence, forgiveness, and God's help.

But when done right, there's nothing sweeter than being of one mind and mouth to praise God together. Ask the Lord to make your community like-minded in purpose and passion so you're glorifying Him together.

What can I do, right here, right now, to help encourage a spirit of unity in my church?

God Made Today

This is the day that the Lord has made;
we will rejoice and be glad in it.
Psalm 118:24

No matter what today holds, you can trust that God made it—and you can choose joy. Even if you bomb a project, get reprimanded at work, have a fight with your husband, get another negative pregnancy test, or fall short on cash—God is still good. You may receive a bad medical report or make a mistake as a friend or parent, but God is still on the throne.

Regardless of the bad news, cling to the truth that you're loved by the Father who holds the whole world in His hands. He sees you, friend. He understands what you're walking through today. And He's already working all things for your good. These are promises from the Bible you can trust. So when you are struggling to be glad about today, focus on God's goodness and be glad in *it* instead.

What can I do, right here, right now, to choose joy in difficult days?

Resist and Submit

Submit yourselves, therefore, to God.
Resist the devil and he will flee from you.
JAMES 4:7

To resist the devil is to be active. Resisting the devil means vigorously withstanding, striving against, or opposing his schemes. We're instructed to resist the trouble and temptations he brings, but don't miss the first part of the verse. Submitting to the Lord is the key.

Ephesians 6 tells us to put on the full armor of God, providing us powerful and divine protection. The devil can't win when he knows we're standing in the strength of our Father. And putting on the armor shows our steadfastness to aggressively resist as we trust God.

Be quick to pray when life comes barreling at you. Prayer is how you draw on His strength to resist. Dig into the Word and let its truths encourage your heart. Hide in the shadow of God's wings and let Him guide your next step. Resist. . .and the devil will flee.

What can I do, right here, right now,
to effectively resist the devil's schemes?

The Call to Be Holy

As obedient children, not fashioning yourselves according to the former lusts in your ignorance, but as He who has called you is holy, so you be holy in all manner of conduct, because it is written, "Be holy, for I am holy."

1 Peter 1:14–16

It takes self-discipline to say *no* to your former habits and hangups—the ones that led you down the path of destruction. There may be muscle memory involved, so saying *yes* feels easy. It's known and comfortable. But when you become a believer and those sins are forgiven, the right path forward is one of righteousness. And it may take God's strength and your steady resolve to walk in holiness with your choices.

Where do you need to make this change? Where are you holding on to those former things? God wants you to be holy because He is holy, and you are His daughter. Confess and repent, and then ask for His help.

What can I do, right here, right now, to choose holiness?

Joy from Abiding in Christ

"I am the vine; you are the branches. He who abides in Me, and I in him, the same brings forth much fruit. For without Me you can do nothing."

John 15:5

To abide in Christ means you have a close, personal, active relationship with Him. It's not superficial. Instead, it's a daily pursuit in every area of your life and essential for rightly relating with the Lord. It's knowing your salvation is secured through Jesus. It's experiencing abundant joy. It's an authentic connection. Abiding means you are saved by grace.

In that truth you'll find the strength and wisdom to navigate the ups and downs of life. It's what gives you purpose in your work and home life. When you say *yes* to Jesus and lean on Him, you live life through the lens of faith. You experience joy and bring glory to God.

What can I do, right here, right now, to ensure I am abiding in Christ?

Blessings for Obedience

"If you are willing and obedient, you shall eat the good of the land. But if you refuse and rebel, you shall be devoured by the sword." For the mouth of the LORD has spoken it.

ISAIAH 1:19–20

The reality is that you have free will. You can repent of your sinfulness and accept the free gift of salvation, or you can refuse Jesus' invitation and continue living in the ways you deem best. You can also let your choices reflect obedience to God's commands for a righteous life, or you can cling to old habits. The Word is full of reminders that He blesses obedience.

Every day, choose to follow the Lord, trusting His plan in your personal life and in your career. Spend time in the Bible. Develop a healthy and active prayer life. And let nothing keep you from doing God's will so you "shall eat the good of the land."

What can I do, right here, right now, to follow God's will and ways first?

Caring for Yourself

What, do you not know that your body is the temple of the Holy Spirit, who is in you, whom you have from God, and you are not your own? For you were bought with a price. Therefore glorify God in your body and in your spirit, which are God's.

1 Corinthians 6:19–20

Friend, be purposeful in making decisions about your body. Think about it. The Father created you. Jesus redeemed you. And the Holy Spirit lives in you. So, how you treat *you*—including your body—matters deeply to the Lord. In all you do, remember you were bought with a price and you're not your own. Focused and faithful living pleases God and points others to Him—and this includes honoring God with our body.

Whether on the job or at home, you have a responsibility to treat your body with thoughtfulness. Let others see your faith at work in the ways you care for your physical and spiritual self.

What can I do, right here, right now, to treat my body better?

Gifts to Share

Having then differing gifts according to the grace that is given to us: whether prophecy, let us prophesy according to the proportion of faith; or ministry, let us attend to our ministering; or he who teaches, on teaching; or he who exhorts, on exhortation; he who gives, let him do it with simplicity; he who rules, with diligence; he who shows mercy, with cheerfulness.

Romans 12:6–8

Did you know God put giftings in you, just as He did for those around you? When you join together in community, everyone's different gifts work in tandem, supporting one another in a beautiful way. It's like the gears of a clock—each piece is needed for things to work well.

That's why church is important. You have a gift your church family needs, and your fellow church members have gifts you need. The weekend may be time to catch your breath from a busy week, but when you embrace church, you will find encouragement and be energized as well.

What can I do, right here, right now, to become an integral part of my local church?

Showing Support

Bear one another's burdens, and so fulfill the law of Christ.
GALATIANS 6:2

While we're personally responsible for many things ourselves, Paul tells us to also be a support to those around us. We are called to come alongside friends and family when they're struggling, offering help through kindness and wise counsel. We should consider it our privilege and responsibility to assist them in carrying the weight of trials and temptations that feel too heavy. Community can be such a powerful tool for believers.

Who in your life is in the midst of a heavy battle right now? Be it a coworker, a classmate, a neighbor, or someone close to you, how can you help in meaningful ways? Even on your busiest days, how can you show compassion and care for them? It's not your job to fix things, but you can be a breath of fresh air. You can cheer them on. And you can make sure they don't feel isolated in their challenges.

What can I do, right here, right now, to show support to someone I know?

Standing in His Strength

We are troubled on every side, yet not distressed; we are perplexed, but not in despair; persecuted, but not forsaken; cast down, but not destroyed.

2 Corinthians 4:8–9

Truth: Life will beat you up. It's hard, and there is no escaping the dark valleys our human experience brings. It may be broken relationships that weigh you down or health struggles that won't go away. Maybe your financial situation is a constant stressor or you're working through challenging issues in therapy. Maybe your ideas for a new venture can't seem to get off the ground or your boss is hypercritical of your work performance.

But you have God on your side, and the joy of the Lord is your strength. As you press into Him, let His presence bring comfort and peace as He leads you through each trouble, step by step. By faith you will overcome and conquer.

What can I do, right here, right now, to stand in God's strength and overcome?

Turning to God First

"Therefore, also now," says the LORD, "turn even to Me with all your heart, and with fasting, and with weeping, and with mourning."

JOEL 2:12

God wants to be the one you cry out to when facing battles. He wants your tears and heartaches. He wants your eyes focused solely on Him as provider and healer. The Lord wants all of your heart, not just bits and pieces, here and there. He wants you surrendered, confessing and repenting, desiring a deeper relationship. And rather than pouring yourself into work or keeping your personal life in overdrive as a distraction from what's really going on, you are invited to turn to Him for help.

What keeps you from going to the Lord first? What keeps you from trusting Him when you're overwhelmed? Who or what do you go to instead of your heavenly Father? There's no one who loves you more—no one more willing and able to help—than God.

What can I do, right here, right now, to trust God in every circumstance?

Hearing and Doing

But He said, "Yes, rather, blessed are those who hear the word of God and keep it."
Luke 11:28

One of the ways we show God our loyal love is to not only read His Word, but also to make every effort to keep it. It's through scripture we learn about the Lord and His commands for righteous living. We're called to hear it and hold on to it.

What a privilege to read accounts of Bible characters who were richly blessed because of obedience. (Think of Abraham, Joseph, and Job.) We read the words of Jesus' teaching and preaching to both Jews and Gentiles. And we have our own life experiences of His goodness to remind us of how God honors our efforts to follow His directives. Make time every day to dig into scripture so the Holy Spirit can minister to your heart and empower you to do as the Word says.

What can I do, right here, right now, to hear and do what God commands?

Persistent Prayers

And He spoke a parable to them to this end,
that men ought always to pray and not to faint.
Luke 18:1

The encouragement in Luke 18:1 is plain and simple to read, yet harder to obey. Jesus wants us to be persistent in our prayers. We're to pray every time that person or situation comes to mind. And rather than lose hope when it seems the Lord's answers aren't coming quickly enough, we're to keep on asking. We should keep the faith, believing God will respond in the right ways and at the right time.

So don't give up. Don't lose heart. Don't grow faint in your prayers. Instead, bring them to the feet of Jesus each time you remember them. Pray confidently, certain He hears you and is already at work on your behalf. Pray courageously, asking for what you need with a bold belief that you matter greatly to God.

What can I do, right here, right now,
to be confident and persistent in my prayers?

He Is Good All the Time

And tear your heart and not your garments, and turn to the Lord *your God, for He is gracious and merciful, slow to anger and of great kindness, and relents from doing evil.*

Joel 2:13

It's important to remember that your Father is good. . .all the time. Hold on to this powerful truth when you feel angry at Him or are struggling to see His hand moving in your situation. Cling to this fact when you're tired in the battle and feel all alone. Every time you feel unseen or unloved by God, let this beautiful reality settle your spirit.

Your Father is unrivaled in every way. He is gracious to those who love Him. He is full of compassion, understanding the complexity of your heart. The Lord doesn't get mad easily, and when He does, it's a righteous anger without sin. He extends unmatched kindness to His children, always willing to meet you right where you are. And His ways are entirely holy.

What can I do, right here, right now, to remember that God is always good?

Daily Awareness of God

Rejoice always. Pray without ceasing.
Give thanks in everything, for this is the will
of God in Christ Jesus concerning you.
1 THESSALONIANS 5:16–18

Is God expecting you to literally pray without stopping? If so, how are you supposed to find time to interact with family and friends? How are you going to get any work done or take time to travel and explore the world? How can you attend class or professional development training?

Thankfully, Paul is telling believers to live each day with an awareness of God. We should remember He's with us and actively moving in our circumstances. He's aware of what's in our hearts and stirring in our spirits. And when worry or fear begin to creep in, we should be quick to give those struggles to the Lord in prayer and choose peace. It should be our first response to depend on Him and not on self.

What can I do, right here, right now,
to help me be always aware of God's presence?

Living Peaceably

Do not repay evil for evil to any man.
Provide honest things in the sight of all men. If it is possible, as much as it lies in you, live peaceably with all men. Do not avenge yourselves, dearly beloved, but rather give place to wrath, for it is written, "Vengeance is Mine. I will repay," says the Lord.

ROMANS 12:17–19

Part of your purpose as a believer is to be an agent of peace—which is not an easy role to walk out, especially when your feathers get ruffled. Maybe your friend didn't come through as promised, or you discovered your man's betrayal, or your coworker took credit for your work. It's circumstances like these that can birth deep hurt and anger. But God says revenge is not yours to exact.

This isn't a call to be a doormat. Healthy boundaries and hard conversations are important. But keep short accounts and trust God to bring justice in His timing and in His ways.

What can I do, right here, right now, to maintain a peaceful heart?

Be Aware, Not Afraid

Be sober, be vigilant, because your adversary the devil walks about like a roaring lion, seeking whom he may devour. Resist him, steadfast in the faith, knowing that the same afflictions are experienced by your brothers who are in the world.

1 Peter 5:8–9

While it's difficult to grasp this truth at times, it doesn't change the fact that the devil is constantly looking for ways to cause us harm. His anger is really directed much higher, but Satan knows God is untouchable. So instead, the devil goes after the Lord's beloved—His sons and daughters. That means because you're a believer, you are in the enemy's crosshairs.

Be aware, but don't be afraid. With God's help, you can resist Satan by remaining faithful, trusting your Father for strength and wisdom. It's inevitable—the devil will bring trials and temptations, but you're not alone. The Lord will show you the way out.

What can I do, right here, right now, to be aware but not afraid?

He Understands

For we do not have a high priest who cannot be concerned with the feeling of our weaknesses, but was in all points tempted as we are, yet without sin. Therefore let us come boldly to the throne of grace, that we may obtain mercy and find grace to help in time of need.

Hebrews 4:15–16

There is no issue or struggle you can pray about that the Lord won't understand. While on the earth, He was tested in every way that you may find yourself tested throughout your life. . .so He gets it.

Jesus isn't without compassion and sympathy for what challenges come your way. So rather than shy away from praying about things that feel too personal, you're invited to boldly come to the throne of grace. You don't have to be embarrassed, because the Lord has a full and complete understanding—and there is mercy in abundance waiting for you. He will help you in your time of need.

What can I do, right here, right now, to trust the Lord with my personal struggles?

Watch and Pray

"Watch and pray, that you do not enter into temptation. The spirit indeed is willing, but the flesh is weak."

Matthew 26:41

Temptation will come; there's no doubt about it. Not only has the Bible been crystal clear in setting this expectation, but you've been navigating it since as far back as you can remember. And alone, it's difficult at best to turn away from those things that entice. It takes God's help to stand strong against fleshly desires and harmful cravings. And the best thing we can do is pray.

Being tempted isn't a sin, but acting on those urges is. Jesus said to watch and pray so you don't enter into wrongdoing. Refuse to flirt with what can bring you disaster at work or at home. A fleeting moment of happiness with sin isn't worth it. You may have every good intention to turn away, but only God can fortify that resolve and give you victory through faith.

What can I do, right here, right now, to prepare myself to fight temptation?

Praying for Your Enemies

"But I say to you, love your enemies, bless those who curse you, do good to those who hate you, and pray for those who despitefully use you and persecute you, that you may be the children of your Father who is in heaven."

MATTHEW 5:44–45

Sometimes it's hard to imagine praying for those who are mean-spirited toward us, choosing to offer blessings rather than curses, regardless of their mistreatment. But it's God's desire and command. More times than not, His economy is drastically different than that of the world. And His expectations for believers seem upside down compared to what feels normal.

Are you angry at your boss or coworker for hurtful comments? Is your roommate being unkind? Does your boyfriend make you feel like an inconvenience? Are your parents being critical of your path forward? Take today's scripture to heart and pray for them anyway, and watch God work in your heart and theirs.

What can I do, right here, right now, to faithfully pray for those who hurt me?

Fight or Be Still?

And Moses said to the people, "Do not fear. Stand still and see the salvation of the LORD, which He will show to you today. For the Egyptians whom you have seen today, you shall never see them again. The LORD shall fight for you, and you shall remain silent."

EXODUS 14:13–14

God expects you to navigate difficulties with His strength and guidance. He wants you to be engaged and moving forward as He opens and closes doors. Sometimes that means you should initiate the hard conversation at work or be the strong one in the rocky relationship. But there are other times when God's plan is for you to let Him battle on your behalf.

How do you know the difference? Ask God to unveil your role in each circumstance. Listen for His still, small voice. And always err on the side of faith, letting the Lord course correct if needed. He always has your best interest in mind.

What can I do, right here, right now, to know my role in difficult circumstances?

It's About Motives

You ask and do not receive because you ask wrongly, that you may spend it on your lusts.

James 4:3

The issue in James 4:3 is *motive*. Are you praying for things to fulfill your selfish desires or for what glorifies the Lord? Think about it: There's nothing wrong with asking God to make you successful in your career. It's okay to want to do well. But if your desire for success is simply to have the best of everything, that motive isn't holy. If success gives you a larger platform to share the gospel, that desire glorifies Him.

James warns us not to ask wrongly, because we won't get what doesn't bring God glory. Instead, we should pray for strength in struggles. Ask for wisdom and discernment in spades. Tell the Lord about your need for comfort and peace to combat fear and worry. Let God know you trust Him to give you what is best.

What can I do, right here, right now, to maintain pure and holy motives in prayer?

Investing Yourself in Church

Then those who gladly received his word were baptized, and the same day about three thousand souls were added to them. And they continued steadfastly in the apostles' doctrine and fellowship and in the breaking of bread and in prayers.

Acts 2:41–42

The powerful thing about investing yourself in a church is having the opportunity to grow together. Worshipping corporately, witnessing commitments and baptisms, watching growth in numbers, hearing God's Word, engaging in fellowship—being part of a church family is beautiful. It may also be messy at times, and inconvenient for your busy schedule. And it may keep you from enjoying a day to sleep in. But God has called us to be in community with other believers, regardless.

What has your experience been with church? What keeps you from being more involved? In what ways might getting more involved in church be a good thing? Ask God to make community something that excites and encourages you.

What can I do, right here, right now, to invest myself in my church?

Even Though He Knows

"For your Father knows what things you have need of before you ask Him."
Matthew 6:8

Let's be careful to not read Matthew 6:8 as reason to not pray. While it's true that God knows everything that worries and weighs you down at this moment, He still wants to hear from you. He wants you to share your struggles in authentic ways. What bothers you matters to your Father. God deeply desires to have a personal relationship with you, and for your voice to rise up into the heavens and into His throne room regarding anything and everything.

When relationships are wearing you out or your schedule feels too overwhelming or you just had a really dreadful day, talk to God. Tell Him what you need—what you want. Unpack everything with honesty. Watch as His peace and comfort surround you and let you know everything will be okay. . .because He holds you in His hand.

What can I do, right here, right now, to pray authentically to God?

Being the Hands and Feet

Therefore, "If your enemy is hungry, feed him; if he is thirsty, give him a drink. For in so doing you shall heap coals of fire on his head." Do not be overcome by evil, but overcome evil with good.

Romans 12:20–21

As believers, we're called to love others. We're called to be the hands and feet of Jesus to a broken world. And God has called us to show kindness and generosity, even when it's the last thing on our mind. When we walk this out with purpose and passion, it brings glory to the Father in heaven. That is our greatest goal.

How and why is it challenging to meet the needs of others? What keeps you from cultivating a servant's heart? What factors make this feel impossible? Ask God to open your eyes to any barriers that might be creating fear and keeping you from stepping out of your comfort zone.

What can I do, right here, right now, to embrace the call to love others and glorify God?

God Is Greater

For if our heart condemns us, God is greater than our heart and knows all things.

1 John 3:20

Simply put, God is greater than your mistakes and missteps. He's greater than any guilt or shame that plagues you. He has full understanding of your thoughts and motives in every situation, even when you're engaging in sin. And He wants you to know that He is greater still. What a blessing!

In the Bible, *heart* usually refers to a person's emotions, feelings, will, and desires. John is reminding his readers that the Lord is greater than all of these, and that truth should offer comfort to us as believers. So when you mess up and make a bad choice, take comfort in knowing that God's love is greater than any condemnation you may feel inside. Be quick to confess to the Lord and move on rather than letting those weighty feelings hold you down.

What can I do, right here, right now, to remember that God is greater than my mistakes?

Illuminating the Right Way

Your word is a lamp to my feet and a light to my path.

Psalm 119:105

Just like you use a flashlight to walk through the dark, the Word of God lights your life. It illuminates the right way to go and the best path to take. If you will let it, scripture will be what guides you through the ups and downs of your human experience. Its instruction will keep you from harm, and when you do encounter those difficult moments, it will bring encouragement and comfort.

There are lots of worldly voices giving you their best advice—often with the greatest intentions—but they can't compete with the power and precision of God's Word. Whether they're challenges at work, frustrations at home, fears of an unknown future, or struggles with decision-making, direction can be found in scripture. There's nothing you'll face here on earth that the Bible doesn't address.

What can I do, right here, right now, to let God's Word be my guiding light through life?

Confessing Sins

If we say that we have no sin, we deceive ourselves,
and the truth is not in us. If we confess our sins,
He is faithful and just to forgive us our sins
and to cleanse us from all unrighteousness.

1 John 1:8–9

Part of living a life of faith is confessing sins. While they've already been forgiven, acknowledging them before God ensures that there's nothing between you and Him. Don't let unrepentant sin block the flow of that relationship. Confessing sin not only wipes your guilty conscience clean, but also makes you aware of the need for a Savior.

Were you disrespectful to a boss? Did you lose your temper with a friend? Have you been lying to a loved one? Are you gossiping behind someone's back? Did an angry word fly out of your mouth during the traffic jam? Even though you're a believer, you still sin. Take today's verse to heart and confess sin right away to clear the air between you and the Father.

What can I do, right here, right now,
to faithfully confess my sins and shortcomings?

Saying No to Sexual Immorality

Flee fornication. Every sin that a man does is outside the body, but he who commits fornication sins against his own body.

1 CORINTHIANS 6:18

Paul is telling the Corinthians to flee all sexual immorality. Just a few verses before this, he reminded them it's the only sin that unites two people together as one, making it even more destructive—and unlike any other kind of sin, this one is against their own body. Believers' bodies house the Holy Spirit and should be used to bring God glory in all things.

The world will tell you differently. It will encourage you to be free, to do whatever pleases you. Culture will offer up countless opportunities to be ensnared in sexual immorality. But God will strengthen you to remain faithful and choose His way above any earthly pleasures. As you seek Him, the Lord will give you the ability to free yourself from the snares.

What can I do, right here, right now, to pursue purity above worldly temptations?

Praying from the Heart

"Therefore, pray according to this manner: Our Father who is in heaven, hallowed be Your name. Your kingdom come. Your will be done on earth as it is in heaven. Give us this day our daily bread. And forgive us our debts, as we forgive our debtors. And do not lead us into temptation, but deliver us from evil. For Yours is the kingdom and the power and the glory forever. Amen."

MATTHEW 6:9–13

Called the Lord's Prayer, Matthew 6:9–13 offers a model for believers to use as they talk to God. It helps readers understand what to include in prayer. But speaking this word-for-word daily and calling it good falls short of the Lord's hope of hearing from you. He's more interested in listening to what's on your heart than simply hearing you recite formulaic prayers without emotion.

From your personal struggles to your deep concerns for the world—and everything in between—just talk to God. He wants to hear from you!

What can I do, right here, right now, to really pray from my heart?

In His Great Love

But God demonstrates His love toward us,
in that while we were still sinners, Christ died for us.
Romans 5:8

We cannot even begin to understand the depth of love God has for us. As humans, we're incapable of grasping it. But His compassion is so great that He made a way for us to be in a right relationship again through His Son Jesus. He did all the work.

Many people think that before they can accept the gift of salvation, they must clean up their act. So they try—in their own strength—to be "good enough." But that's a wild goose chase. Best laid plans fail. God made the way, *His* way, "while we were still sinners." Friend, you can come to Jesus as a mess and His arms will be wide open. You're accepted just as you are.

What can I do, right here, right now,
to accept and appreciate God's great love?

Through the Lens of Faith

And do not be conformed to this world, but be transformed by the renewing of your mind, that you may prove what is that good and acceptable and perfect will of God.

ROMANS 12:2

As you grow in your faith, trust the Holy Spirit to transform your mind. It's His job to deepen the roots of faith and change you from the inside out. Each time you open your Bible or spend time in prayer, He will mature you in all the right ways. Watch as the things of the world grow strangely dim and you long for eternal treasures instead.

That doesn't mean you lose interest in loving others well or you care nothing for a job well done. But you now do so through the lens of faith. Your desire is to do the Father's work by reflecting His goodness into each day and every interaction.

What can I do, right here, right now, to partner with the Holy Spirit?

Let Your Love Be Real

Let love be without hypocrisy.
Hate what is evil; cling to what is good.
ROMANS 12:9

Let your love be real. This is part of your purpose. God calls us to love. So let it be authentic, caring for others with a pure heart. Doing so will help shine the love of Christ into their day. Be mindful, assuring you aren't faking it to manipulate or gain control of a situation. And remember it's because God first loved you, that you can love those around you well and in His strength.

How are you challenged today? While it may be easy to love some, what person in your community is hard to love and why? Ask the Lord to help you pursue what is good with fervor, including loving the unlovable. Rather than holding onto offenses or sitting in judgment, ask God to bring perspective and soften your heart for others. Ask Him for the strength and compassion to love with sincerity.

What can I do, right here, right now, to love others with a pure heart?

Being a Team Player

"If My people who are called by My name shall humble themselves and pray and seek My face and turn from their wicked ways, then I will hear from heaven and will forgive their sin and will heal their land."

2 Chronicles 7:14

The world feels crazy these days. There are wars and rumors of wars. Political parties are at each other's throat constantly. There seems to be more violence and evil now than just a few years ago. And while you alone cannot fix the chaotic circumstances, you can play a role in the healing of our land.

Every time you turn from sinful ways, humbling yourself in prayer and seeking God above all else, it makes a difference. And imagine what could be possible if other believers did the same. Encourage those around you to step up as you commit to being a team player yourself. Choose to live humbly, seek righteousness, and be prayerful.

What can I do, right here, right now, to help bring healing to the land?

Joy of the Lord

Then he said to them, "Go your way, eat the fat, and drink the sweet, and send portions to those for whom nothing is prepared. For this day is holy to our Lord*. Do not be sorrowful, for the joy of the* Lord *is your strength."*

Nehemiah 8:10

You can find joy in the world. It may be success in the classroom, recognition in the boardroom, or a great night's sleep in the bedroom. It may come from a new or restored relationship. No doubt there's joy to be found in people and circumstances, but only when things are good. People will frustrate and situations will change.

Joy that comes from the Lord, however, is unmatched. His joy in the believer is consistent, regardless of the hills and valleys of life. When you focus on all God has done and all He promises to do, joy will naturally follow. And that joy will give you strength to manage what life brings your way.

What can I do, right here, right now, to find joy in the Lord?

God Listens

"Then you shall call on Me and you shall go and pray to Me, and I will listen to you. And you shall seek Me and find Me, when you shall search for Me with all your heart."

Jeremiah 29:12–13

As women, we want to be seen and heard. We want to know that what we feel matters. We want someone to help us talk through difficult circumstances. But too often, we focus on finding people *here* to be good listeners. They may be helpful for a while or in certain situations, but at some point, they'll let us down.

God is always available. You can call on Him 24/7/365. Scripture confirms that when you seek God wholeheartedly, you'll find Him. He'll listen to every detail weighing on your heart. There's nothing God doesn't understand completely, and it's His strength, compassion, and wisdom that will guide you through the valley.

What can I do, right here, right now, to make God my sounding board and guide?

Constant Companion

You have surrounded me behind and before and laid Your hand on me. Such knowledge is too wonderful for me; it is high; I cannot attain it. Where shall I go from Your Spirit? Or where shall I flee from Your presence?

PSALM 139:5–7

In those moments where you feel all alone, know that God's presence is with you always. He goes before you. He walks next to you. And He is behind you too. You're literally surrounded by the Lord on every side, all the time.

As you're having the hard conversations, He's there. When the unexpected phone call comes, He is with you. When heading into a big test or intimidating meeting, the Lord is right there. No matter what your day holds, God's presence is a constant companion. There's no place you can go where He is not already present. Be encouraged. You're so deeply loved that the Lord never leaves your side.

What can I do, right here, right now, to recognize God's constant presence?

Be a Doer of the Word

But be doers of the word and not hearers only, deceiving your own selves.

JAMES 1:22

The book of James is known for offering practical advice about living a righteous life. In its pages, the author doesn't mince words. When he says to be doers and not just hearers, James is telling believers to demonstrate their faith by being obedient to God's commands. There is a blessing that comes to those who hear the Word and then walk it out.

The Bible isn't just a nice book, full of interesting stories and good suggestions that can sit collecting dust on a shelf. It's not meant to be just thought-provoking—the Bible demands action. It's designed to supernaturally transform the heart of believers so they can live faithfully with passion and purpose. It's a collection of inspired commands that's meant to be obeyed.

What can I do, right here, right now, to act on what the Bible teaches?

Created to Live Purposefully

For You have possessed my inward parts.
You have covered me in my mother's womb.
I will praise You, for I am fearfully and
wonderfully made. Marvelous are Your
works, and my soul knows that very well.
PSALM 139:13–14

Friend, settle in your heart right now that you were created *on* purpose and *for* a purpose. You are not a mistake or the result of a cosmic explosion. Instead, God personally formed you. He knit you together, choosing your unique gifts and talents. While at times it may not feel this way, the truth is that you're fearfully and wonderfully made.

When you're struggling to feel good enough to complete your responsibilities or calling, remember that God doesn't make mistakes. He wasn't having an off day when He created you. And you weren't made to be perfect in every way. That's impossible. Instead, you were created to live purposefully.

What can I do, right here, right now, to accept that I am fearfully and wonderfully made?

The Discipline to Be Humble

For through the grace given to me I say to every man who is among you not to think of himself more highly than he ought to think, but to think soberly, according to the measure of faith God has dealt to every man.

Romans 12:3

It takes discipline to be humble. Maybe you are excellent at your job, setting all kinds of company records. Maybe you are a culinary genius and people rave about the meals you put on the table. Or maybe you're wise beyond your years, making you the go-to for sound wisdom and advice. Stay humble and recognize your gifts and talents come from the Lord alone.

God will not bless the prideful. Instead, He promotes the humble in heart. Choose to live your life in ways that bless others and bring glory to the Father. And be grateful for His goodness and how it brings favor to you.

What can I do, right here, right now, to cultivate genuine humility?

How to Live and Love Well

Be kindly affectionate to one another with brotherly love, preferring one another in honor, not slothful in business, fervent in spirit, serving the Lord, rejoicing in hope, patient in tribulation, continuing persistently in prayer, distributing to the needs of the saints, given to hospitality.

Romans 12:10–13

Do you ever wonder about your purpose as a believer? Does it matter how you live or how you treat others? The answer is. . .yes!

Romans 12:10–13 is a good reminder of what God expects. We're told to love one another with true devotion and to be quick to put the needs of others above our own desires. Rather than being slack, we're to be fervent about serving the Lord. We are to be joyful and hopeful, standing strong in challenging times. We should be persistent in prayer, and kind and generous toward others. No matter where we are or what we're doing, we should embrace who God has created us to be.

What can I do, right here, right now, to live and love according to God's plan?

Calling Out to God

"This is what the LORD—its Maker, the LORD who formed it to establish it, the LORD is His name—says: 'Call to Me, and I will answer you and show you great and mighty things that you do not know.'"

JEREMIAH 33:2–3

As God's beloved, you're invited to call out to Him, anytime and anywhere. Whether in the middle of the project, in the airport on a business trip, camping in the mountains, walking into a hard conversation, or sick in bed, your Father wants to hear your voice. Do you need insight or perspective? Do you need a hefty dose of hope? Are you lacking wisdom or discernment? Are you afraid and worried? Do you need the comfort of His presence? Are you confused or overwhelmed?

Let God answer you with great and mighty things that you don't yet know. Let Him meet your needs as the great provider. Call out to God and He will respond.

What can I do, right here, right now, to confidently call out to God for help?

Stand Your Ground

And being found in appearance as a man,
He humbled Himself and became obedient
to death, even the death of the cross.
PHILIPPIANS 2:8

Jesus stepped out of heaven and into a sinful world to save us. He endured pain, scorn, hatred, abuse, and even an excruciating death on a cross. At any point, Jesus could have raised His hand and tapped out. He could have said, "Enough is enough," and called off the grand plan. There were legions of angels in the heavens waiting for His command to intervene. But Jesus knew what needed to happen to save mankind from eternity without God, and He showed great self-discipline to stay the course.

Let this encourage you to stand your ground too. In circumstances where you want to give up or give in, just stand. Humble yourself before the Lord and ask for strength and endurance. Let your resolve be known and do what God requires by faith.

What can I do, right here, right now, to follow God's will and stand strong?

Nothing Compares

For I consider that the sufferings of this present time are not worthy to be compared with the glory that shall be revealed in us.

Romans 8:18

Suffering is just part of life, and there's no way to avoid it. From birth to death, at home and at work, and on every day of the week, we're susceptible to heartache. So, thinking that believers are immune to trouble is dangerous. Jesus said, "I have spoken these things to you, that in Me you might have peace. In the world you shall have tribulation, but be of good cheer: I have overcome the world" (John 16:33). And in today's verse, Paul tells us why we can have that hope.

Even our very best moments on earth can't come close to the experience of God's glory in eternity. We can endure the temporary suffering now because we're promised lasting goodness in heaven. Friend, choose to embrace this divine perspective that emboldens your faith in suffering.

What can I do, right here, right now, to put my suffering into perspective?

God Is Your Help

I will lift up my eyes to the hills. Where does my help come from? My help comes from the L*ORD, who made heaven and earth.*

PSALM 121:1–2

When life feels overwhelming and anxiety sets in, be quick to lift your eyes toward the heavens. Go right to God and pray for help. Ask for wisdom and discernment to know the next right step. Ask for strength to stand strong through the storms. Pray for peace to reign in your heart as you walk through the challenges. And let God be your comfort—your safe place. The Father will meet you in the mess and bring you through safely. Every time you need help, no matter the issues, He will be there.

What battles are raging in your life right now? Where are you worried or afraid? As a believer, you're invited to run right to God with confidence that His help will be exactly what's needed, and at the perfect time.

What can I do, right here, right now, to trust God's help?

Unashamed of the Gospel

For I am not ashamed of the gospel of Christ, for it is the power of God for salvation to everyone who believes, to the Jew first and also to the Greek. For in it the righteousness of God is revealed from faith to faith, as it is written, "The just shall live by faith."

Romans 1:16–17

We are called to confidently and boldly proclaim the truths found in God's Word. We can trust that what was inspired by the Holy Spirit and written thousands of years ago is still real and relevant today. We're to also live the gospel out at work and at home every day, certain our faith in it isn't misplaced.

Being ashamed of the gospel can look like hesitating to share your faith, holding back from mentioning Jesus in conversations, or avoiding standing up for biblical truth out of fear of rejection or judgment. This is not God's desire for our lives. He wants us to stand firm for truth—and He will gladly provide strength and courage when we ask.

What can I do, right here, right now, to let faith dominate how I live each day?

Showing Kindness and Love

Let brotherly love continue. Do not forget to entertain strangers, for by this some have entertained angels unawares.

HEBREWS 13:1–2

This is a great reminder to show kindness and generosity to everyone—a homeless person on the street, someone in the store, a cranky neighbor, a demanding boss, family and friends who drive you nuts at times. God wants His children to show love. His desire is that we demonstrate patience. This is a high calling and one of foremost importance to the Father's heart.

It's cool to think you may have encountered an angel dressed as a stranger. Let this always be in the back of your mind when your annoyance arises. Before you speak rudely because of being inconvenienced, take a breath. Bite your tongue. Hold off speaking your mind in hurtful ways. Instead, let compassion be your default response.

What can I do, right here, right now, to show love and respect to everyone?

For a Season

In this you greatly rejoice, though now for a season, if need be, you are in heaviness through many different temptations, that the trial of your faith, being much more precious than gold that perishes, though it is tried with fire, might be found to praise and honor and glory at the appearing of Jesus Christ.

1 PETER 1:6–7

Remember that your suffering is for a season. Every issue you're battling at work is temporary. The challenges at home have an expiration date. The struggles in your marriage won't last forever. And the health scares and financial stressors will come to an end. Yes friend, the heaviness you're experiencing will subside.

When you press into God and trust Him for comfort and resolution, you'll find that. Though you've been tried by fire, your faith will delight the Lord. You will emerge victorious. God will bless your perseverance and you'll be encouraged to stand strong in the next season too.

What can I do, right here, right now, to remember this is just a season?

Loving God with All

"And you shall love the Lord *your God with all your heart and with all your soul and with all your might."*
Deuteronomy 6:5

This often feels like a super-sized command that's unattainable for mere mortals. Just how can you be expected to love God with *all* your heart and soul and might? The answer? You simply can't. It's impossible. That's why you need—we all need—a Savior.

So in those moments where you just cannot do what is expected, ask the Lord to empower you for the task. Remember that as your faith grows, so does your ability to love God better. As you invest in your relationship with Him, your love will also deepen. And as you're eager to be the woman He's called you to be—spending time in His Word and prayer and self-denial—your faith will mature, and your love will become more steadfast. Never forget: This is a journey.

What can I do, right here, right now, to love God more each day?

Saying No to Fleshly Desires

Now the works of the flesh are evident, which are these: adultery, fornication, uncleanness, lewdness, idolatry, witchcraft, hatred, dissensions, jealousies, wrath, strife, rebellions, heresies, envyings, murders, drunkenness, carousing, and the like, of which I tell you before, as I have also told you in time past, that those who do such things shall not inherit the kingdom of God.

GALATIANS 5:19–21

The fleshly desires listed in these verses sound familiar, don't they? Are you seeing them in the world today in greater measure? These sinful and lewd activities do not please God, and so as believers, we should turn away from them quickly and decisively. But it requires His help to choose holiness. In our humanity, we're weak.

Let your life be marked by righteousness. When others are giving in and compromising, be one who stands strong in God's strength. Keep your eyes focused on what's eternal rather than what's earthly.

What can I do, right here, right now, to turn away from fleshly and worldly desires?

Afflictions Strengthen Faith

For our light affliction, which is but for a moment,
is working for us a far more exceeding and eternal
weight of glory, while we look, not at the things
that are seen, but at the things that are not
seen. For the things that are seen are temporal,
but the things that are not seen are eternal.
2 Corinthians 4:17–18

Many times, we find ourselves looking for the EJECT button when life gets hard. We want off the roller coaster and onto solid ground. We want to lock the door, crawl under the covers, and escape into a favorite book or movie. From a broken relationship or being overworked at work or crumbling under the weight of expectations, we're overwhelmed. But we're missing the point.

God uses every affliction to strengthen our faith. Walking through them with the Lord brings spiritual maturity. So don't try to avoid them like the plague. Remind yourself that He is allowing them for your good and His glory. . .and simply trust.

What can I do, right here, right now,
to see my suffering through God's eyes?

The Reward of Faith

"Do not fear any of those things that you shall suffer. Behold, the devil shall cast some of you into prison, that you may be tested, and you shall have tribulation ten days. Be faithful to death, and I will give you a crown of life."

Revelation 2:10

While Revelation 2:10 was part of the letter written by Jesus to the church in Smyrna, it's packed with two powerful points about Christian living for today.

First, it reminds us that the devil is alive and active, constantly launching attacks on those who love the Lord. Even more, he's creating an atmosphere of hostility and hatred toward God here and now. Can't you see humanity's continuing shift from Christian to worldly values?

Second, this verse comforts us because we're assured the Father knows our struggles and promises eternal life in the end. Our steadfast faith through the rough spots will be rewarded.

What can I do, right here, right now, to keep an eternal perspective on earthly struggles?

Making Time to Pray

And in the morning, rising up a great while before day, He went out and departed to a solitary place and prayed there.
MARK 1:35

Even Jesus needed to rise early and find a quiet place to pray, and He was the Son of God. So don't beat yourself up for struggling to make time for prayer with work or family distractions swirling all around. Just plan to find sacred space where you can connect with your Father in meaningful ways.

Some rise early and curl up in their favorite chair. Others make time to pray on the drive to and from work. Maybe you're a night owl and have your time with God after hours. Or maybe you find time with Jesus during your walk or run. The important thing is to make prayer a priority so your load will be lightened and your heart encouraged for what lies ahead.

What can I do, right here, right now, to make prayer a priority?

He Will Never Leave Your Side

Who shall separate us from the love of Christ?
Shall tribulation, or distress, or persecution,
or famine, or nakedness, or peril, or sword?
. . . No, in all these things we are more than
conquerors through Him who loved us.
Romans 8:35, 37

Sometimes we feel all alone in our difficult seasons. It can seem as if we've been deserted, trying to figure things out without anyone's help. And while we know there are friends and family who love us, and that God is always with us, demanding times are often lonely times. But then we read these verses from Paul and realize those feelings of isolation aren't true.

Nothing can separate us from His love. Even in our darkest hours, the Lord is fully present. And because of that, we can have strength to stand in faith and weather every storm. As believers, we're not alone. Our Father will never leave our side, not even for a moment.

What can I do, right here, right now,
to live in the truth of God's presence?

A Powerful Collective

Now we exhort you, brothers, warn those who are unruly, comfort the feebleminded, support the weak, be patient toward all men.

1 Thessalonians 5:14

Church can be a powerful collective of believers equipped to spur each other on in faith. It's an opportunity to receive encouragement to battle on and ignite hope that God will make a way. It introduces us to other like-minded people on the same journey of righteousness, navigating the mountaintops and valleys of life. And it teaches us to love others well.

Chances are, your life is hectic these days. It may feel like there aren't enough hours to get through your to-do list. And weekends may be the only time you have to catch up on sleep. But when you choose to make church attendance a priority anyway, God will bless your commitment. You will find a support system there to help you through this world.

What can I do, right here, right now, to adjust my schedule to make church attendance a priority?

Being Intentional

But the end of all things is at hand. Therefore, be sober and watch in prayer. And above all things have fervent love among yourselves, for love shall cover the multitude of sins.

1 PETER 4:7–8

It takes self-discipline to be watchful. This doesn't happen without intentionality.

We must be deliberate to love and forgive others. We must choose to slow down and use discernment. We should be present in conversations rather than letting our minds drift to our to-do list. Instead of being laser-focused on work, let's consciously notice what's happening around us. Let's take self-inventory, making sure we're engaging in the right ways and at the right times.

Remember that the world doesn't revolve around you. Every day, make time for God—and time to connect with purpose to those you care about. Relationships always take priority.

What can I do, right here, right now, to be intentional with those I love?

Godly Friendship

Rejoice with those who rejoice,
and weep with those who weep.
Romans 12:15

Part of your purpose here on earth is to be a good friend. Community is important to God, and He often uses other people to bring us much-needed encouragement. Friends help to process life through the lens of faith. They step in to help us when we can't help ourselves. Sometimes they challenge us, bringing a fresh perspective to our situations. Not only do we need solid and godly friends, but we need to be solid and godly friends for others.

Who are the friends you cherish? Name those special women who take the time to rejoice and weep with you. They are blessings from the Lord and a gift each day! Take a moment to thank Him for placing them in your life, then ask that He equip you to serve them in significant ways as well.

What can I do, right here, right now,
to make and grow Christian friendships?

Purpose in Our Pain

Blessed be God, even the Father of our Lord Jesus Christ, the Father of mercies and the God of all comfort, who comforts us in all our tribulation, that we may be able to comfort those who are in any trouble, by the comfort with which we ourselves are comforted by God.

2 Corinthians 1:3–4

What a beautiful picture 2 Corinthians 1:3–4 paints for believers. God brings comfort to us in our suffering so we can be a comfort to others. He teaches us what encouragement looks like. And as we experience it from the Father, we then learn how to console those around us. We can offer reassurance to the weary because He first offered it to us.

Friend, there's much purpose to our pain. It's not for naught. God uses every bit of it for our benefit and His glory. And Paul tells us it's also recycled to bless others in their own battles.

What can I do, right here, right now, to support others in their suffering?

Caring for Others

That there should be no schism in the body, but that the parts should have the same care for one another. And whether one part suffers, all the parts suffer with it, or if one part is honored, all the parts rejoice with it.

1 Corinthians 12:25–26

Believers are called to have sympathy and compassion for one another. We're expected to depend on and be dependable. And we shouldn't be okay with letting the spirit of division fester. If someone is suffering, we're all called to join in the suffering. If honored, we should share that honor. This is a beautiful image of the church. God put us together with great thought and intentionality. We're one.

Knowing that, make sure you take time from your busy schedule to be present with other believers this week. Be sensitive to those who are struggling. Reach out with celebration when necessary. Just as you'd like to be seen and known, so do others.

What can I do, right here, right now, to have meaningful connections with other believers?

Reaping in Joy

Those who sow in tears shall reap in joy. He who goes forth and weeps, bearing precious seed, shall doubtless return with rejoicing, bringing his sheaves with him.

Psalm 126:5–6

The concept of sowing and reaping is found all over the Bible. Often, the rule is that the more seed is planted, the more fruit is harvested. But it also implies that there's a waiting period involved. Reaping doesn't happen overnight or with little effort. It requires steadfast consistency on the part of believers.

Be encouraged by Psalm 126:5–6. This excellent news will benefit every area of your life—relationally, spiritually, and emotionally. When your heart is burdened and you continue taking that pain to God, trusting that He'll hear and act, you'll receive a reward for faithfulness. You will be blessed with joy for perseverance. And the welcome harvest from your sowing will be wonderful.

What can I do, right here, right now, to sow with perseverance so I can reap in joy?

Integrity in Church

Now I beseech you, brothers, by the name of our Lord Jesus Christ, that you all speak the same thing and that there be no divisions among you, but that you be perfectly joined together in the same mind and in the same judgment.

1 Corinthians 1:10

While Paul was asking the believers in Corinth to be united as they shared the good news of Jesus with others, this verse also applies to us today. A church divided won't grow in numbers or in spiritual maturity. You may have seen chaotic divisions take place in person or read about other troubled churches in the news. Unfortunately, without a spirit of unity, earnest prayer, and God's protection, division can become a reality.

Pursue integrity. Reject gossip or negativity. Decide you won't sit in judgment, letting bad feelings fester. Ask God to make you a woman of character who helps the message of Jesus spread and grow.

What can I do, right here, right now, to help my church grow?

You Can Do All Things

I can do all things through Christ who strengthens me.

Philippians 4:13

Philippians 4:13 doesn't promise you'll win every game, outsmart the stock market, or blow past the confines of your humanity. It's not a guarantee of superhero powers, nor of a problem-free life. Instead, Paul is discussing what believers can do to faithfully endure life's difficulties through Jesus' strength.

When your finances fail, or you get fired from the job, or you discover your husband's betrayal, press into God. When you're struggling to find your footing from grief, go right to Him in prayer. When the test results reveal a scary diagnosis, ask the Lord for help and hope. Regardless of the heavy circumstances swirling around you, you—as a believer—can do everything you need to do through Christ, who strengthens you.

What can I do, right here, right now, to lean into God for strength in trials?

Giving God the Glory

The LORD *is my strength and my shield.*
My heart trusted in Him, and I am
helped. Therefore my heart greatly rejoices,
and with my song I will praise Him.
PSALM 28:7

Think about who God is to you. How has He helped you navigate the ups and downs of life? How has the Lord encouraged your heart in times of trouble? In what circumstances have you seen Him rescue or restore you from weariness? How has God strengthened you or given unexpected wisdom? In what ways have you experienced His peace? How have you felt His comfort?

These are the circumstances that should drive us to joy. Seeing God's hand move in our life should fill us with tearful thanksgiving and joyful gratitude. Have you shared heartfelt praise with Him? Have you expressed your appreciation? Friend, never miss an opportunity to give God the glory!

What can I do, right here, right now, to give God glory for His goodness?

Slow to Anger

He who is slow to anger is better than the mighty,
and he who rules his spirit than he who takes a city.
Proverbs 16:32

Scripture says believers should be slow to anger. For many, this is a tall order. It's challenging to be calm when travel plans get messed up or when a coworker takes credit for your idea. Remaining composed when you're disrespected or treated unfairly is difficult. And when it seems life keeps throwing punches, staying relaxed doesn't often come easily. Yet God expects believers to control their anger rather than letting it control them.

He knows every situation weighing on you right now. He understands the self-control it requires to navigate hard circumstances without a blowup. So why not have an ongoing conversation with God throughout the day, asking for peace and perspective? Rather than letting it pile up, process those maddening moments with Him, so anger doesn't come easily.

What can I do, right here, right now, to make sure my anger is controlled?

Compassion for the Faithless

For we ourselves also were sometimes foolish, disobedient, deceived, serving various lusts and pleasures, living in malice and envy, hateful, and hating one another. But after that the kindness and love of God our Savior toward man appeared, not by works of righteousness that we have done, but according to His mercy He saved us, by the washing of regeneration and renewing of the Holy Spirit.

TITUS 3:3–5

Let's remember we were once wretched in our sins too. Whether directed at a neighbor, coworker, or family member, there's no place for a self-righteous attitude toward unbelievers. We should demonstrate compassion instead, praying regularly for the lost. The Lord found us in our transgressions and saved us by grace. So let's reveal the blessings of a life of faith rather than passing judgment.

In humility, let's show unbelievers the kindness of Jesus—the kindness He showed toward us when we were still drowning in our own sin.

What can I do, right here, right now, to be humble toward unbelievers?

God's Word Is Pure

Every word of God is pure; He is a shield to those who put their trust in Him.

Proverbs 30:5

Every single word God speaks throughout the Bible is pure and trustworthy. It's fully truth because He, as the author, is incapable of mistakes. And God's Word is the final authority. From the promises to the revelation to the testimonies, it's infallible and immaculate and untainted. You can trust scripture to offer direction when you're lost, strength when you're weak, wisdom when you're confused, and comfort when you're hurting. Since God's Word is pure, it has the power to purify believers. And it's a shield of protection to all who trust in Him.

How does this truth challenge you today? What makes it hard to trust that every word of God is pure? What keeps you from looking to scripture as a roadmap for life? Take every concern to the Lord and ask Him to solidify His truth in your heart today.

What can I do, right here, right now, to confirm to myself that God's Word is pure and perfect?

Praying in the Busy

In my distress I called on the Lord *and cried to my God. He heard my voice out of His temple, and my cry came before Him, even into His ears.*

Psalm 18:6

No matter what you're dealing with today, cry out to the Lord for help. Life is big at times and full of bumps, and we need the Father's love to steady our anxious hearts. And while you may want to figure things out on your own, don't even try. Go right to God and tell Him everything weighing heavy on you today.

Your schedule might be packed with business meetings and travel. You may have the expectations of after-work commitments. Or you may be craving the chance to zone out and hide from the chaos. But friend, it's worth your time to pray amid the busy. Be it a quick prayer or in depth, He's listening and ready to help.

What can I do, right here, right now, to make prayer a priority even when I'm busy?

The Godly Shall Suffer

Yes, and all who will live godly in Christ Jesus shall suffer persecution.

2 Timothy 3:12

If your goal is to live in ways that please God, then buckle up. Wake up each day and pray, putting on the full armor of God, as detailed in Ephesians 6:13–17. Because you *will* suffer persecution. But you're never alone. God is with you through the highs and lows and will give you everything needed to stand strong as long as you put your full faith in Him.

Be ready to flex your faith muscles. Expect difficulties. Assume that hardship is coming. But also embrace joy and peace, trusting that since God allowed difficulty, He will overcome it with you. And He only allows what is for your good and His glory. You're not alone.

What can I do, right here, right now, to not be caught off guard when hardship comes?

Working Together

For as we have many parts in one body and all parts do not have the same function, so we, being many, are one body in Christ, and each one is a member of the others.

ROMANS 12:4–5

Every Christian woman has her own special and unique God-given gifts to share with other believers. And we're to appreciate what each person brings to the table. This is the kind of diversity we should celebrate with passion because it's what makes the church function as God intended.

Be careful not to assume your gifts are better than anyone else's. Each person has an important role to play—through teaching, hospitality, or administration, these giftings work together, benefiting the whole body of Christ. Let this also be a sweet reminder that you hold immense value as a woman of God. The church needs the goodness God put into you!

What can I do, right here, right now, to better serve Jesus' church?

What Faith Looks Like

Trust in the L*ORD, and do good, so you shall dwell in the land and truly you shall be fed. Delight yourself also in the* L*ORD, and He shall give you the desires of your heart. Commit your way to the* L*ORD. Trust also in Him, and He shall bring it to pass.*

PSALM 37:3–5

Trust God. Do good. Delight in the Lord. Commit your life to Him. Psalm 37:3–5 unpacks what a life of faith looks like. When you accept Jesus as your personal Savior, this is how you live righteously.

So how are you doing with this? Which part comes easier, and what feels almost hopeless? Remember, the life of a believer is a relationship—between you and God. And it's impossible to live faithfully without His help through the Holy Spirit. Before your feet hit the ground each morning, ask for the ability to glorify His name in the way you live, and watch God's goodness unfold.

What can I do, right here, right now, to "trust in the LORD, and do good"?

Knowing the Scripture

Jesus answered and said to them, "You err, not knowing the scriptures or the power of God."
MATTHEW 22:29

Knowing what God's Word says is so important for the believer trying to live a holy life. Unless you do, how can you be certain you're following His will? How can you know the right way to manage conflict in the workplace? How can you navigate challenging relationships with love and truth, so it pleases the Lord? And how can you make choices that align with His commands?

Like a fish out of water, a believer without daily time in God's Word struggles to thrive. We need divine nourishment each day, distinguishing truth from lies as our faith matures. We need His Word to renew and transform our mind. And when we open the pages of God's Word, the Lord will meet us there with fresh insight and understanding. He will honor the time we invest in knowing the scripture.

What can I do, right here, right now, to make Bible reading a daily desire and habit?

God Restores

He restores my soul. He leads me in the paths of righteousness for His name's sake. Yes, though I walk through the valley of the shadow of death, I will not fear evil, for You are with me. Your rod and Your staff, they comfort me.

Psalm 23:3–4

Let Psalm 23:3–4 bring comfort to your weary spirit today. Never forget the ability God has to restore your soul—something no one nor anything else can match. He alone has the supernatural power to lift the heaviness and replace it with peace.

Are you walking through a dark valley today? Does anxiety have the best of you right now? Is it challenging to not be fearful or worried about certain things? Are you battling mentally and emotionally just to get through the day? Friend, cling to God and let Him lead you through these difficult moments and seasons.

What can I do, right here, right now, to allow God's goodness into my painful circumstances?

Turned to Joy

You have turned for me my mourning into dancing. You have put off my sackcloth and girded me with gladness, to the end that my glory may sing praise to You and not be silent. O LORD my God, I will give thanks to You forever.

PSALM 30:11–12

Where has God turned your deepest pain into joy? Where has He taken your garments of mourning and clothed you with gladness instead? The truth is that when you wholeheartedly seek the Lord's help in your battles, He steps in and changes outcomes in meaningful and beautiful ways. And it fills your heart with gratitude.

Maybe a relationship came to an unexpected end. Maybe you lost a job you deeply enjoyed. Maybe a beloved family member died. Maybe you overextended yourself financially. Maybe your heart's desire didn't come to fruition. Be quick to ask God to intervene and bring hope. Because with that hope comes unyielding joy.

What can I do, right here, right now, to let God turn my pain into joy?

Quick to Listen, Slow to Speak

Therefore, my beloved brothers, let every man be swift to hear, slow to speak, slow to anger. For the anger of man does not work the righteousness of God.

James 1:19–20

Can we be honest and admit it's difficult to be slow to speak when tempers flare? When we feel cornered or offended, we can be quick to defend ourselves. We can let graceless words fly rather than really listening. And in frustration, we can overwhelm others when we lose control of our emotions. These choices don't please God.

As a believer, the goal of your life is to point others to the Lord. Whether in the classroom, the office, the community, or your home, be quick to listen and slow to speak. Breathe in deeply and pray for God's help. Ask questions and let others respond. Then let your words be measured and true.

What can I do, right here, right now, to be sure I listen first then speak respectfully?

His Word and Spirit

Teach me to do Your will, for You are my God.
Your Spirit is good; lead me into the land of uprightness.
Psalm 143:10

God doesn't desire to hide His plans from you. He isn't making you work overtime to unlock the secret code that frees you to learn more. Instead, God has equipped you for deeper understanding. When you seek Him wholeheartedly, you will find Him.

You have been given God's Holy Word as a way to learn what He wants for your life. Whether through a physical Bible or an online app, you can access scripture whenever and wherever. And God has given believers the Holy Spirit, who takes up residence inside them. If you'll let Him, He will lead and direct your days.

Together, these two invaluable resources will open your eyes and transform your heart to live in ways that benefit you and please God.

What can I do, right here, right now,
to learn more about God and His plans for me?

Compromises

Let your eyes look directly ahead, and let your eyelids look straight before you. Ponder the path of your feet, and let all your ways be established. Do not turn to the right hand or to the left; remove your foot from evil.

PROVERBS 4:25–27

It takes great discipline to keep your eyes focused on the path God has revealed to you. Every day, you will face temptations. Maybe you'll be tempted to slack off at work or entertain the attention of someone outside your marriage. Maybe you'll be tempted to spend money unwisely or pass someone else's ideas off as your own. The list of possibilities is, unfortunately, endless.

Be careful to walk in righteousness, even when compromises may seem small and insignificant. Trust that God has your good in mind when He tells you how to live. Other people may never find out what you've done behind closed doors, but God always sees.

What can I do, right here, right now, to live with integrity and without compromise?

Don't Give Up

"For My thoughts are not your thoughts, nor are your ways My ways," says the Lord. *"For as the heavens are higher than the earth, so are My ways higher than your ways and My thoughts than your thoughts."*

Isaiah 55:8–9

Reading the Bible can be confusing. Jesus often talked in parables, and sometimes, the meaning of His words is challenging to understand. Certain books of the Bible talk about heavenly creatures and things in the future that are hard to comprehend. And there are commands that feel unattainable. But rather than throw in the towel, we should find resources to help.

Consider reading scripture in different translations to see if one connects better. Read commentaries or work through Bible studies from trusted sources. Ask the Holy Spirit for revelation. Talk to a spiritual mentor or a theologically sound pastor. You may not understand everything this side of heaven, but God will bless your persistence in studying.

What can I do, right here, right now, to be a better student of God's Word?

Exchanging Fear for Faith

You will keep him whose mind is steadfast on You in perfect peace because he trusts in You.
Isaiah 26:3

When life feels overwhelming, one of the hardest choices to make is intentionally focusing on God's faithfulness instead of our stressful circumstances. Maybe your default button is going into fix-it mode, trying to figure things out yourself. Maybe you binge-watch TV or eat comfort food to numb the anxiety. Or maybe you're just rendered ineffective and end up emotionally paralyzed, unable to move forward.

God promises peace to those who keep their mind steadfast on Him. Rather than shut down or jump into hyperactivity, why not pray? Let the Lord know what's causing worry or fear and He will settle your spirit. Ask for His intervention and thank God for His goodness toward you. And as that exchange from fear to faith takes place, something beautiful will happen: His perfect peace will wash over you, confirming everything will be okay.

What can I do, right here, right now, to choose faith over fear?

Your Life Preaches

"You are the light of the world. A city that is set on a hill cannot be hidden. Nor do men light a candle and put it under a bushel, but on a candlestick, and it gives light to all who are in the house. Let your light so shine before men, that they may see your good works and glorify your Father who is in heaven."

MATTHEW 5:14–16

Whether at work, at home, at church, or in your community, remember that your life preaches, one way or the other. Your words and actions either point others to God in heaven, or lead people in the wrong direction. Your choices can be full of kindness and generosity, or they will demonstrate selfish, carnal living.

It's out of the heart that you live each day. So spending time in God's Word and in prayer, and investing in your church family, allows His goodness to pour out in how you act and speak.

What can I do, right here, right now, to shine the light of Jesus into my world?

His Exceeding Abundance

Now to Him who is able to do exceedingly abundantly above all that we ask or think, according to the power that works in us, to Him be glory in the church by Christ Jesus throughout all ages, world without end. Amen.

Ephesians 3:20–21

God is all-powerful. He's all-knowing. And whatever we can imagine or hope that He's capable of doing in our lives, the truth is that there's so much more than that. The Father is limitless in every way; we are unable to comprehend all He is and can do. We just can't dream that big.

So, friend, pray big and bold prayers. Be sure your motives are aligned with His character and then ask! Do you want to own a company? Do you want a large family? Do you want a health problem to disappear? Do you want to travel the world to share the gospel? With God, you can ask and expect exceeding abundance!

What can I do, right here, right now, to confidently pray big and bold prayers?

Deep in Your DNA

My son, attend to my words; incline your ear to my sayings. Do not let them depart from your eyes; keep them in the midst of your heart. For they are life to those who find them and health to all their flesh.

PROVERBS 4:20–22

What are your thoughts about the Bible? Is it a book written by men and therefore flawed and untrustworthy as a whole? Is it filled with creative stories, many of which aren't true? Are there helpful parts and others that are irrelevant? Is your Bible untouched and collecting dust on your bookshelf?

The truth is that God's Word is alive and active. Every writer was inspired by God as he wrote the words God gave him. And when you take it seriously—believing it is the Lord's full counsel—you'll be blessed in meaningful ways. Wherever you are and whatever you're doing, let the Bible guide your steps. Let the richness of scripture settle deep into your DNA, bringing you life and health.

What can I do, right here, right now, to embrace the whole Bible as God-inspired?

Trusting Brings Joy

Our soul waits for the L*ORD*. *He is our help and our shield. For our heart shall rejoice in Him, because we have trusted in His holy name. Let Your mercy, O* L*ORD*, *be on us, as we hope in You.*

Psalm 33:20–22

Do you struggle with trust? Chances are that the answer is *yes*. People have let you down. Dependable processes and procedures have failed. And what was once reliable no longer is. Anchoring faith in anything the world offers only leads us to sadness and pain. But God is forever faithful and stubbornly steadfast in His promises.

Notice the psalmist says he's joyful *because* he trusted in the Lord. By faith, he hoped in God's goodness while waiting for His guidance. The choice to trust was deliberate. Friend, no matter what you're facing right now, anchor your trust in God alone and let joy fill your anxious heart as you watch for His hand to move. His love never fails.

What can I do, right here, right now, to pursue the joy that results from trusting God?

God Will Meet Your Needs

"Therefore I say to you, do not worry for your life, what you shall eat or what you shall drink, or yet for your body, what you shall put on. Isn't life more than food and the body more than clothing?"
MATTHEW 6:25

There are lots of situations that can lead to anxiety. Maybe you're stressed about the money to cover medical bills or pay for car repairs. Maybe the job you love doesn't pay enough to meet your needs, and you're at a crossroads about your future. Maybe you'd like to eat better, but the cost of cleaner foods is too high. But scripture tells us not to worry.

God knows your needs and promises to meet them. You can trust that! But also have faith He'll meet your needs according to His plan and timing. God's answers won't always be your answers. But faith reminds you His heart for you is good, and His plans are better than anything you can imagine.

What can I do, right here, right now, to trust God will faithfully meet my needs?

Comes from Above

Every good gift and every perfect gift is from above and comes down from the Father of lights, with whom there is no variation or shadow of turning.

James 1:17

As believers who receive God's goodness every day, we should respond with a heart of thanksgiving. James says that everything good comes from above. Do you recognize that in your own life?

When you achieve a challenging goal, thank God for giving you the strength to make it happen. When you find the money in your budget to pay the bills, recognize God's provision. When you find a wonderful new friend, be grateful that He created the friendship. When you land the job of your dreams, thank the Lord for His favor. You may have worked hard, made wise decisions, and exhibited perseverance, but even that ability came from God. Create an attitude of gratitude that always points to His goodness.

What can I do, right here, right now, to recognize God's hand in my life?

An Agent of Unity

Behold, how good and how pleasant it is for brothers to dwell together in unity!
PSALM 133:1

Unity is important to God. He knows the value a strong community brings to the lives of believers. Scripture says it's good and pleasant. And when we can't find common ground with one another, we become preoccupied with all the wrong things. We're stuck in offense rather than thriving in togetherness. In the end, we miss the blessing unity can bring in the boardroom, the classroom, or the living room.

But it really matters in your church community. We need harmony to function well as a Christ-centered collective, bringing encouragement to each other and effectively sharing the gospel. We need unity to follow God's command to love and serve. Without healthy and constructive interaction, our faith is hindered by worry and stress. Are you an agent of unity in your circles? If not, what needs to change?

What can I do, right here, right now, to be an agent of unity?

Knowing He Is God

Make a joyful noise to the Lord, all you lands. Serve the Lord with gladness; come before His presence with singing. Know that the Lord, He is God. It is He who has made us, and not we ourselves; we are His people, and the sheep of His pasture.

Psalm 100:1–3

There is joy and relief when you truly embrace that God is God, and you are not. Friend, you don't have to figure everything out yourself. You don't have to have all the answers. And rather than carry the weight of work and home responsibilities on your shoulders, you can lay each struggle at His feet. The Lord promises to help navigate the challenges that feel too heavy to carry alone.

Let this truth stir a joyful noise within you. Live each day serving God from a place of gladness, knowing that He reigns supreme. And let your delight be evident through a heart of thanksgiving.

What can I do, right here, right now, to find joy in God's sovereign lordship?

Letting It All Out

The righteous cry, and the Lord hears and delivers them out of all their troubles. The Lord is near to those who are of a broken heart and saves those who have a contrite spirit.

Psalm 34:17–18

What a blessing to know that God draws close to us when our hearts are broken. There is no better source of comfort than His presence. And if we'll cry out when hard moments hit, the Lord will surround us with His perfect peace.

As you pray, let it all out. Be honest about your feelings and invite God into your mess. In silent prayers or wordless groans, trust that He knows exactly what's going on inside you. The Holy Spirit will advocate for you. The Lord hears you and promises to deliver you out of the trouble that's causing pain. So rest, knowing you are in good hands.

What can I do, right here, right now, to let God's presence heal my heart?

A Loving and Humble Heart

Be of the same mind toward one another. Do not think about high things, but associate with men of low position. Do not be wise in your own opinions.
ROMANS 12:16

We may sometimes feel like we are better than others. Maybe we earned the highest test score or received a coveted promotion over our coworkers. Perhaps we have a nicer car or a trendier apartment. Maybe our culinary skills are a cut above. Perhaps we know more scripture than others in our circles. Be careful: When we decide we're better than those around us, God is displeased and trouble follows.

Humility draws people together. It opens the door to authentic friendship and makes us approachable. Because the Lord's plan is for us to love others well, we should let Him cultivate a loving and humble heart in us. When people feel seen and accepted, everyone wins.

What can I do, right here, right now, to live with a humble heart?

Called to Holiness

For God has called us not to uncleanness but to holiness. Therefore, he who despises this despises not man but God, who has also given us His Holy Spirit.

1 THESSALONIANS 4:7–8

It takes a steady resolve to choose holiness over worldliness, because what's offered in the here and now is enticing. Sin is often fun. It offers pleasure, albeit short term. Chances are, you have family members, coworkers, or friends who actively pursue wrong. Our world is so bad that we can become desensitized to sin. But as a believer, you can trust the Holy Spirit to put a check in your own spirit when sin comes knocking.

How do you stay disciplined to obey when your flesh calls out for the unclean? Seek God in prayer, asking for strength and wisdom, and read His living and active Word. Then consciously choose to deny yourself, instead pursuing what delights His heart.

What can I do, right here, right now, to make holiness my greatest desire?

Celebrating in Joy

Let them praise His name in the dance; let them sing praises to Him with the tambourine and harp. For the Lord *takes pleasure in His people; He will beautify the meek with salvation.*

Psalm 149:3–4

There are countless reasons to be joyful, thanks to our relationship with the Lord. Rather than seeking happiness—worldly-driven and circumstantial at best—believers can experience lasting joy because of God's goodness. His joy is our strength. It's a fruit that the Holy Spirit carefully matures in us. It's found through obedience to His commands. And it's the promise of God's continual presence that gives us cause for rejoicing.

You might choose to dance or praise Him with music. You could recount His kindness in prayer or share testimonies of God's hand in your life. However you do it, be sure to praise the Lord. He's worthy! Not only does it delight His heart, it strengthens your faith—it keeps your eyes focused on eternal, rather than earthly, things.

What can I do, right here, right now, to celebrate God's goodness in my life?

Called to Put On

Put on, therefore, as the elect of God, holy and beloved, hearts of mercies, kindness, humbleness of mind, meekness, long-suffering, being patient with one another and forgiving one another if any man has a quarrel against any. Even as Christ forgave you, so you also do.

Colossians 3:12–13

In Colossians 3:12–13, Paul reminds the church to stay unified, show compassion, and be quick to pardon offenses against one other. The church is God's elect, set apart and called to "put on" a holy way of living. Compassion, kindness, humility, gentleness, patience, and forgiveness should mark their lives. And friend, it should also be what marks your life.

What keeps you from clothing yourself with these things? Which in the list above feels impossible to achieve at work? Which ones are challenging to put on at home? Do any of them feel unattainable in your church community? God knows where you're struggling and will empower you if you ask.

What can I do, right here, right now, to put on a holy way of living?

Delighting in God's Word

Blessed is the man who does not walk in the counsel of the ungodly or stand in the way of sinners or sit in the seat of the scornful. But his delight is in the law of the LORD, and on His law he meditates day and night. And he shall be like a tree planted by the rivers of water that brings forth its fruit in its season. His leaf also shall not wither, and whatever he does shall prosper.

PSALM 1:1–3

God promises to prosper and bless those who follow His commands. Delighting in and meditating on the Word brings God's favor into your work and home life. And as you choose to live in righteousness, the Lord is honored. Let His Holy Spirit do the work at hand, maturing the fruit of faith in you in purposeful ways.

Today, ask for the wisdom of God's Word to guide you into the richness of His goodness.

What can I do, right here, right now, to find joy and delight in my Bible?

God Is Your Source

"Do not fear, for I am with you. Do not be dismayed, for I am your God. I will strengthen you. Yes, I will help you. Yes, I will uphold you with the right hand of My righteousness."

Isaiah 41:10

God is your source for every good thing. And when you look to Him above all else, you will see this truth playing out in real time in your life. Whether you need energy for the week, or patience for parenting, or wisdom at a crossroads, there's no lack with God. Circumstances may feel confusing, but you don't need to be dismayed. Instead, you can lean into Him and He'll uphold you.

The Lord wants you to live in victory, standing confident in your faith as you traverse the mountaintops and valleys. What do you need to get through today? What challenges ahead are creating worry? God is your source for life here on earth, so call on Him.

What can I do, right here, right now, to trust God with everything?

Keeping Marriage Honorable

*Marriage is honorable in all and the bed undefiled,
but God will judge fornicators and adulterers.*

Hebrews 13:4

Whether you're married now or you're hoping to be someday, be the kind of wife who honors the covenant made with God and her husband. It may seem obvious, but the world is working overtime against traditional marriage. And unless you draw a line in the sand, asking God to protect your union as you work through issues, temptation can creep in. And it will wreak havoc.

God authored marriage and uses it to grow us and bless us. It can be very difficult at times—you might even want to throw in the towel. You may be tempted to meet your needs in unbiblical and unhealthy ways. But your decision to stay faithful, working out your differences, is something God will honor. Because marriage is honorable in all.

**What can I do, right here, right now,
to respect God's institution of marriage?**

His Word Endures Forever

"The grass withers, the flower fades,
but the word of our God shall stand forever."
Isaiah 40:8

Simply stated, everything earthly (including people) will wither and fade. Nothing here lasts forever. This world—and everything in it—has an expiration date. Whether it's a sweet relationship, or an exciting new job, or a fat savings account, it will eventually end. So, placing your happiness and faith in anything earthly is unwise. It will prove to be unfulfilling.

But as a believer, you can find comfort knowing God's promises are everlasting and unfailing. His words of hope and healing will endure through every up and down life brings. You can count on the Lord to do what He said He'd do, without fail. And when everyone and everything else lets you down, you can be confident that God will never fail you. In the best of times and the worst of times, your Father in heaven will make good on His Word.

What can I do, right here, right now, to increase my trust in God's never-failing Word?

What Has God Done?

Then our mouth was filled with laughter and our tongue with singing. Then they said among the nations, "The Lord *has done great things for them." The* Lord *has done great things for us, of which we are glad.*

Psalm 126:2–3

What "great things" has God done for you? Did He open the lines of communication in a relationship that felt hopeless? Did He connect you with a new friend after you'd prayed for months? Did the Lord inspire a doctor with a different protocol that's proving to be life-changing? Did your work just get recognized by the boss, who's now talking promotion?

Because scripture says that all good things come from God (James 1:17), be sure to recognize His hand moving in your life. Be quick to give God glory for the joy you're experiencing. It's all because of His greatness. Thank Him for blessing you in ways that remind you of His matchless love.

What can I do, right here, right now, to recognize God as the source of all blessing?

His Strength in Your Weakness

And He said to me, "My grace is sufficient for you, for My strength is made perfect in weakness." Therefore, I will boast most gladly even more in my weaknesses, that the power of Christ may rest on me.

2 Corinthians 12:9

How is God's strength made perfect in your weakness? Your inability is an opportunity for Him to display His greatness. Where your strength gives out, His steps in. Your faith deepens because your hope is in God to come through. He is all you need when you feel weak.

Is it hard to admit where you're lacking? Are you embarrassed by feeling inadequate in your relationships, on the job, or at home? Friend, God doesn't expect you to be superhuman. He knows where you're struggling. Surrender those places into His hands and let the Lord's strength bring the support you need. God's grace is sufficient.

What can I do, right here, right now, to admit my weakness and lean into God's strength?

Only One God

For there is one God and one mediator between God and men, the man Christ Jesus, who gave Himself as a ransom for all, to be testified in due time.

1 Timothy 2:5–6

The world says there are many gods and many paths leading to eternal life. They say Jesus was just a good man—or maybe even a myth. Many people believe the way to claim a spot in heaven is to do good things: Volunteer in your community! Give money to charity! Go to church! But none of these ideas or actions is correct.

Scripture is clear that there's only one God, a trinity of Father, Son, and Spirit. The second member of this Trinity, Jesus, willingly came into the world to die on the cross to pay the price for our sins. He made the one way for us to be right with God. He was and is the mediator, reconnecting us with the Father. And once we accept this truth, the Holy Spirit lives inside us, growing our faith and empowering us to live holy lives.

Don't let the world mislead you on this very important truth.

What can I do, right here, right now, to enhance my belief in the singular nature of God?

Sweet Spirit of Joy

Let all those who seek You rejoice and be glad in You, and let those who love Your salvation say continually, "Let God be magnified."

Psalm 70:4

When pursuing God with fervor, you'll find yourself marked by a sweet spirit of joy and gladness. This beautiful change in you may be unexplainable by your unbelieving family, friends, and coworkers. But scripture clearly links seeking the Lord and experiencing joy.

Be the kind of woman who not only runs after God wholeheartedly, but also approaches Him with a grateful heart. Whether you need strength for challenges at work or at home, seek out His help. It's from here that joy spills out. As you trust the Lord, seeing His goodness manifest in your circumstances, you'll overflow with thanksgiving. This joy will change you from the inside out.

What can I do, right here, right now, to seek God in wholehearted gratitude?

Having One Mind

Finally, be all of one mind, having compassion for one another, love as brothers, be sympathetic, be courteous.

1 PETER 3:8

Sometimes we as Christians forget we're on the same team. As the church around the world, we have shared goals and responsibilities. But when we get caught up in bickering or judgment, that team spirit begins to break down. We lose focus. Rather than sharing the gospel with passion, serving together with purpose, and loving one another with perseverance, we become ineffective.

Friend, don't do anything that creates disunity. Instead, be a team player in your church community, always helping to foster the "one mind" mentality. Advocate for harmony, so you can be part of a unified people who point to God with their actions. As you love people well, an environment is created for Him to work in the hearts of others.

What can I do, right here, right now, to be a better team player at my church?

The Best Place for Hope

You are my hiding place and my shield; I hope in Your word.

Psalm 119:114

The sweetest, most powerful place to find hope is in God's Word. From Genesis to Revelation, you'll discover strength and encouragement for your weariness. You will find the case for confident faith in the words of Jesus. You will see testimonies to bolster your expectation of His goodness.

If you need a dose of courage or perspective, open God's Word. If you're looking for comfort and peace, make time to dig into scripture. There's no better place to go if you are lacking strength for the struggle.

Are you seeking hope in the world or in the Word? There's only one place (one *Person*) that can meet you in discouragement and reignite your faith.

What can I do, right here, right now, to ensure my hope is found in God's Word?

Be Still and Know

"Be still and know that I am God. I will be exalted among the nations; I will be exalted in the earth."
Psalm 46:10

Psalm 46:10 is more than a simple instruction to be quiet and still in God's presence. While doing so is a beautiful surrender to the Lord, the call is to stop responding in frantic ways. It's to choose peace over panic. Rather than going crazy over circumstances and desperately trying to fix things yourself, take a deep breath, take a step back, and surrender those anxious feelings to God. Look only to Him for help and hope.

Having faith means you believe the Lord is with you. You trust He's all-powerful and all-knowing. You're confident in His goodness and holiness. When you combine these truths with a steadfast belief in God's sovereignty, you will "be still and know." Then you can exhale anxiety and breathe in hope.

What can I do, right here, right now, to be still and know?

A Humble Heart

Let nothing be done through strife or boastfulness, but in lowliness of mind let each esteem others better than themselves.

Philippians 2:3

As believers, we're called to be humble with a servant's heart. We're told to love others and show compassion and concern for their well-being. Rather than thinking of ourselves as "better than," God says to wholeheartedly put others first. We're to love people sacrificially and authentically, letting your words and actions speak directly to their heart. When you do, you're living out your purpose and delighting the Lord at the same time.

The reality: This is a challenging way to live! Sometimes you may not feel like serving others. Sometimes they may not "deserve" it. But that doesn't change God's expectation. Whether we're loving an aging parent or a cranky neighbor or a demanding boss, how we serve others points people back to God.

What can I do, right here, right now, to not think of myself as better than others?

Joy in God's Presence

You will show me the path of life.
In Your presence is fullness of joy; at Your right hand there are pleasures forevermore.
PSALM 16:11

As you walk out your faith every day with God—letting Him direct your steps on the path of life—the fullness of joy you'll experience will be unending. There is something so powerful about giving up the top spot and letting God lead. You will know the gift of true joy. You'll discover what it means to be content. You will find rest. His presence will become your greatest desire and comfort.

Your life will always be busy, but practice choosing God's will and ways over your own. Pray about everything. Dig into the scriptures daily. And watch how your joy increases and perseveres no matter what comes your way. Expect the fullness of joy as you invest in the Lord.

What can I do, right here, right now, to follow God's will and ways?

Making God Visible

Beloved, if God so loved us, we also ought to love one another. No man has seen God at any time. If we love one another, God dwells in us and His love is perfected in us.

1 John 4:11–12

Just like we cannot see the movement of wind, we cannot see God. He is spirit, and our eyes can only focus on material things. In our human condition, it's impossible for us to observe the Lord in action. But we can see His divine fingerprints all over our circumstances. We can demonstrate His love to others. We can be part of His plan to support, inspire, and attract those around us.

Since God loves you, you should love others. Choose to be a blessing to your coworkers. Show kindness to a stranger on the street corner or a neighbor next door. Reassure the heartbroken and embolden the downcast. Make God visible.

What can I do, right here, right now, to make God visible?

Confident About God

I will love You, O Lord, *my strength. The* Lord *is my rock and my fortress and my deliverer, my God, my strength, in whom I will trust, my shield, and the horn of my salvation, and my high tower.*

Psalm 18:1–2

The psalmist knew who God was to him. Thousands of years after he wrote, you can feel the joy of his words. He wasn't wondering if the Lord was good. He wasn't hoping God would come through in the end. There was no crossing of fingers, guessing at God's role in his life. Instead, the writer knew that God was his rock, fortress, deliverer, strength, shield, salvation, and high tower. The psalmist was confident!

What about you, friend? Who is God to you? How does your relationship with the Lord make you joyful? How is God a delight to you? Do you love God with all your strength?

What can I do, right here, right now, to increase my confidence in who God is to me?

Walking in the Spirit

This I say then: walk in the Spirit,
and you shall not fulfill the lust of the flesh.
GALATIANS 5:16

"Walk in the Spirit" describes the way believers should live. It's how we're called to travel through each day. Because we're saved by grace, the Holy Spirit goes to work in us, transforming our heart to be more like His. Walking in the Spirit means we seek His direction and willingly accept His influence over our thoughts, choices, and actions. And it means we turn from our fleshly and self-centered desires.

This is a daily decision—sometimes minute by minute—because it goes against the core of our humanity. It's a retraining of what is good and right. We must always work with the Spirit, allowing Him to empower us to glorify God.

What can I do, right here, right now,
to embrace the Holy Spirit's work in my heart?

Hiding God's Word in Your Heart

With my whole heart I have sought You. O let me not wander from Your commandments. Your word have I hidden in my heart, that I might not sin against You. Blessed are You, O Lord. Teach me Your statutes.

Psalm 119:10–12

In Psalm 119:11, the original Hebrew word rendered *hidden* means to treasure and regard as highly valued. Hiding God's Word in our hearts happens when we spend regular time digging into scripture, meditating on what it says, and memorizing key verses. When we do this, there's a supernatural cleansing that keeps us from unknowingly wandering into sin. The Holy Spirit will nudge us when we need it.

Your schedule may be hectic, full of deadlines and responsibilities. You may be whittling away at your to-do list from sunup to sundown. But taking time to hide God's Word in your heart enables you to walk in righteousness—in ways that please the Lord.

What can I do, right here, right now, to hide God's Word in my heart?

Letting Peace Rule

And let the peace of God rule in your hearts,
to which you also are called in one body. And be thankful.
Colossians 3:15

When the peace of God rules in your heart—especially when life is moving at a breakneck pace—it will reveal the amount of time you've spent in the Word. The more time you invest, the more peace will be present. The less time spent, the more life will be able to shake you. Peace and time spent with God go hand in hand. Work may be overwhelming and home may feel hectic, but His peace has the supernatural ability to hold you steady.

Remember that the Bible says you're to love God with all your heart, soul, and mind. Getting to know Him through the Bible accomplishes that beautifully. Developing a robust prayer life furthers the relationship. The result is a maturity of faith that reflexively trusts God during chaotic circumstances. Do you have that?

What can I do, right here, right now,
to let God's peace rule in my heart?

The Gift of the Holy Spirit

"But the Comforter, who is the Holy Spirit,
whom the Father will send in My name,
He shall teach you all things and bring to your
remembrance all things that I have said to you."
John 14:26

God deposits the gift of His Holy Spirit into the heart of every believer once they accept Jesus as Savior. That means God's presence is a constant—guiding and growing faithful believers into maturity. He never leaves us, not even for a moment.

John 14:26 says the Spirit also provides comfort when needed. He brings to mind key scriptures at the right time. He's the teacher who helps us understand the Trinity and how Father, Son, and Holy Spirit work together in our lives. By God's guidance, by His gentle nudges to do the right thing, we're able to choose ways that please the Lord. The Holy Spirit is a priceless gift for every believer.

What can I do, right here, right now,
to be sensitive to the Spirit's leading?

God Is with You

"Have I not commanded you? Be strong and of good courage. Do not be afraid or be dismayed, for the Lord *your God is with you wherever you go."*

Joshua 1:9

Knowing God is with you is a catalyst for courage and confidence. Let it strengthen you for the hectic workday ahead. Let it bring encouragement when you're discouraged in a relationship. Let it affirm that you are loved when you feel worthless and unimportant. Let it bolster your perseverance for the hard recovery ahead. Let it settle your anxious heart when finances are tight. Knowing the Lord is your constant companion means you don't have to be fearful or depressed.

The reality is that you'll feel stretched at times. Negative feelings will rush in. (You are human, you know.) But here's where you can draw on God's strength. Remind yourself of His power, protection, and presence. He will see you through everything.

What can I do, right here, right now, to stand strong and trust God?

Let There Be Joy!

You are my hiding place. You shall preserve me from trouble. You shall surround me with songs of deliverance.

Psalm 32:7

While God promises to be your hiding place, this doesn't mean your life will be pain-free. Even Christians experience loss, grief, and rejection. You will fail and fall short. You'll suffer from sickness and physical ailments. You'll face stress and anxiety. And while God is *able* to shield or deliver you from all such troubles, He may not. If He doesn't, know that there's a divine purpose for your good and His ultimate glory. You can always trust Him.

James 1:2–3 says we're to count these trials and challenges as "all joy" because He uses them to deepen our faith and strengthen our perseverance. They're how the Holy Spirit matures believers. When the trials hit, know that God will keep you close, guide your steps, and bring you safely through. There is great joy in that truth.

What can I do, right here, right now, to faithfully find joy in my trials?

Friends in Church

Iron sharpens iron; so a man sharpens
the countenance of his friend.
Proverbs 27:17

The friends you make in church play a vital role in your spiritual maturity. They serve many meaningful purposes. They are encouragers in demanding times—"boots on the ground" when you need help. They will always point to God as your source of hope and peace. They become expressions of His love by making Him visible in your life.

You may have amazing coworkers who spur you on. You may have neighbors and classmates who truly love you. And, hopefully, your family invests in you daily. But you also need a church family to challenge the integrity of your faith and keep your eyes focused on eternal things. Seek out friends in church, to help you stay strong and steadfast.

What can I do, right here, right now,
to seek out friendships within the church?

The Call to Comfort

Therefore, comfort yourselves together and edify one another, even as you also are doing.
1 THESSALONIANS 5:11

Part of your purpose on earth is to be a comforter. It's part of God's call for you to love others. You have the ability to offer encouragement to those who are struggling, being a support however you can. And, friend, God has gifted you the ability to make that happen.

Who in your circle of influence needs reassurance? Who needs a cheerleader in their corner? Who needs a fresh dose of hope? Ask God to open your eyes to see those people and to give you courage to step forward. Life is hard, and this world is crazy. Let your heart be tender toward anyone who could use a hand or a hug. Sometimes it's a burden, but it's always a privilege to show Jesus to the hurting.

What can I do, right here, right now, to be a comfort to those around me?

What Do Your Actions Prove?

"If you love Me, keep My commandments."

John 14:15

Words are cheap, but actions offer a true picture of your heart. It's easy to say you care for someone, but do you show it? Are you willing to be inconvenienced to help a friend in need? Will you work longer hours to help a coworker finish a project? Will you take meals, do laundry, or drive carpool to help a neighbor? If you love them, demonstrate it.

The same concept applies to how you respond to the Lord. Jesus said that when you do what He asks and follow the commands He gives, your obedience proves your love for Him. It may not always be easy or convenient, but disciplining yourself to obey speaks volumes. It offers evidence of your true faith and devotion. And the Bible is clear that God blesses obedience.

So, what are you waiting for? Keep the commandments.

What can I do, right here, right now, to better align my words and actions?

A Healthy Respect for God

"Only fear the LORD *and serve Him in truth with all your heart, for consider what great things He has done for you."*

1 SAMUEL 12:24

As believers, we should not be afraid of God. There's no reason to be. We shouldn't be scared into submitting to His will. Instead, when the Bible tells us to *fear* the Lord, it simply means to have a healthy respect. We should have a reverence for God that helps us live in ways that glorify His name. We should respect and obey, worship and praise, trust and surrender.

This life of faith will challenge you every day, but don't be driven by fear that your shortcomings make God dislike you. You're going to mess up—we all do! Don't be afraid of retaliation—the proverbial lightning bolt out of heaven—because you failed. Faith isn't about perfection, but purposeful living.

What can I do, right here, right now, to have a healthy respect for God?

Opening the Word Daily

Seek the LORD *and His strength; seek His face continually.*
Remember His marvelous works that He has done,
His wonders and the judgments of His mouth.

1 CHRONICLES 16:11–12

One of the best ways to seek God's strength and favor is spending time in the Word. You can be purposeful to remember His marvelous works and wonders by reading scripture—all of it, from Genesis to Revelation. For the believer, reading scripture regularly helps you get to know God, His story, and the promises He's made to you.

Here's a challenge to open the Word daily, even if only to read one verse. During your lunch break at work, waiting in the school pick-up line, or relaxing in your comfy chair at home, make time to learn more about the amazing God who loves you deeply. Meditate on His Word, and watch how that simple act of faith transforms your heart and mind.

What can I do, right here, right now,
to seek the Lord and His strength?

Scripture Index

Practical Devotions for Women

Through 28 weeks of readings and related, interactive "life maps," you'll be encouraged to improve your faith life, prayer and Bible time, finances, job, wellness, and more. This book will guide you into a more intentional life—one that honors God and benefits yourself and others for years to come.

Hardcover / ISBN 979-8-89151-043-2